Keto Ninja Foodi Cookbook 2020

Quick and Easy Ketogenic Diet Meals For Your Ninja Foodi Pressure Cooker

By Venante Nowey

Table of Contents

Introduction

Keto diet is in the TOP list of the most in-demand diets in the world. People who follow it for a long time know very clearly that sometimes it can be a boring process to a cooking meal in an ordinary way. This book is a perfect guide in the world of delicious, easy, and fast recipes. The book contains the recipes of breakfast, main dishes, side dishes, lunches, and desserts. All the recipes here are proved in real.

The main feature of every Keto recipe is a high amount of fat and lack of carbs. The most popular Keto-friendly food is meat, fish, full-fat cream, hard cheese, cream cheese, and butter. It is true that the diet implies almost total elimination of carbohydrates. The carbohydrates contain in fruits and vegetables but it doesn't mean that all of them are contraindicated. There are some produces with a small number of carbs; exactly they are very useful for the Keto lifestyle. Such fruits and vegetables are lettuce, swiss chard, collard greens, bok choy, garlic, etc. Each of them contains less them 1 net carb per serving. If we talk about fruits the most Keto friendly fruits are blackberries, avocado, and raspberries. The total amount of net carbs per serving is less than 4 net carbs. All of the best Keto recipes with fruits and vegetables are also in this book. As you have already understood, this cookbook is the perfect find for Keto lovers; nevertheless, there is one more feature of the book – all the recipes were created exactly for Ninja Foodi.

Let's briefly find out what is Ninja Foodi and why it is in the great request and worth to have at home! In September the 5th , 2018 the household innovator Ninja represented a new device that combines the functions of Instant pot and Air fryer. The easily managed appliance can be operated by everyone. The usage of Ninja Foodi is very familiar with using the Instant Pot. The big plus of this machine is that it helps you to manage what is going on inside it. The electronic display window shows you the time that is left and the cooking stage. You can also find a blue light on the display that rotates while pressurizing. Now you don't need to guess anymore when it starts. As it has already said above, Ninja Foodi has a function of Air fryer. Thanks to it, you can easily crisping up the food and therefore enforce the taste of an ordinary meal.

Ninja Foodi is really a miracle invention. It easy to operate, smart, and can cook every your Keto culinary dream. To realize if it true – let's plunge in the world of delicious Keto recipes!

Breakfast Recipes

Parmesan Chicken Wings

Prep time: 10 minutes , Cooking time: 17 minutes , Servings: 2

Ingredients:

- 4 chicken wings
- ½ cup chicken stock
- ½ teaspoon salt
- 1 tablespoon butter, softened
- 1oz Parmesan, grated
- 1 teaspoon garlic powder
- 1 teaspoon minced garlic
- 1 teaspoon dried dill

Directions:

1. Rub the chicken wings with the salt and place in the Ninja Foodi pot.
2. Add chicken stock and close the lid.
3. Seal the lid and cook chicken wings at Pressure Cook mode (High pressure) for 9 minutes.
4. Meanwhile, mix up together the butter, grated cheese, minced garlic, garlic powder, and dried dill. Whisk the mixture until homogenous.
5. When the chicken wings are cooked – make a quick pressure release. Open the lid and transfer chicken wings on the plate.
6. Remove the liquid from the pot and insert rack.
7. Brush the chicken wings with the butter mixture generously and transfer on the rack.
8. Lower the air fryer lid and press the "Broil" mode.
9. Cook the wings for 8 minutes.
10. Enjoy!

Nutrition value/serving: calories 192, fat 12.4, fiber 0.2, carbs 2.4, protein 18

Feta Frittata

Prep time: 10 minutes , Cooking time: 15 minutes , Servings: 3

Ingredients:

- 4 oz fresh spinach, chopped
- 3 eggs, beaten
- 1 oz Feta, crumbled
- ¼ teaspoon white pepper
- ¼ teaspoon salt

Directions:

1. Whisk the eggs well.
2. Stir the spinach in the whisked eggs and add white pepper and salt.
3. After this, add Feta cheese and mix up the egg mixture with the help of the spoon gently
4. Transfer the liquid in the springform pan.
5. Insert the air fryer rack in Ninja Foodi and place the frittata.
6. Lower the air fryer lid and cook frittata at 360 F.
7. Cook for 15 minutes or until the meal is set. Serve it!

Nutrition value/serving: calories 97, fat 6.5, fiber 0.9, carbs 2.2, protein 8

Fish with Sesame

Prep time: 8 minutes, Cooking time: 8 minutes , Servings: 4

Ingredients:

- 1.5-pound salmon fillet
- 1 tablespoon apple cider vinegar
- 1 teaspoon sesame seeds
- ¼ teaspoon dried rosemary
- ½ teaspoon salt
- 1 teaspoon butter, melted

Directions:

1. Sprinkle the salmon fillet with the apple cider vinegar.
2. After this, mix up together the sesame seeds, dried rosemary, salt, and butter.
3. Brush the salmon with the butter sauce generously.
4. Place the salmon on the rack and lower the air fryer lid.
5. Set the air fryer mode and cook fish at 360 F for 8 minutes.
6. Serve it!

Nutrition value/serving: calories 239, fat 11.8, fiber 0.1, carbs 0.3, protein 33.1

Keto Juicy Bacon Strips

Prep time: 5 minutes, Cooking time: 7 minutes, Servings: 2

Ingredients:

- 10 bacon strips
- ¼ teaspoon dried basil
- ¼ teaspoon chili flakes
- 1/3 teaspoon salt

Directions:

1. Rub the bacon strips with the dried basil, chili flakes, and salt.
2. Place the bacon on the rack and lower the air fryer lid.
3. Cook the bacon for 5 minutes at 400 F.
4. Check if the bacon is cooked and cook for 3 minutes more or until you get the desired doneness.

Nutrition value/serving: calories 500, fat 45, fiber 0, carbs 0, protein 20

Cheese Casserole

Prep time: 5 minutes, Cooking time: 22 minutes, Servings: 2

Ingredients:
- 1 oz bacon, chopped
- 2 eggs, whisked
- ¼ cup almond milk
- ½ teaspoon dried basil
- 3 oz Cheddar cheese

Directions:
1. Mix up together the whisked eggs, almond milk and dried basil.
2. Add bacon and transfer the mixture into the springform pan.
3. Grate cheese and sprinkle it over the egg mixture.
4. Place the casserole into the Foodi and set "Air Crisp" mode 365 F.
5. Cook the casserole for 15 minutes.
6. Check the casserole and cook it for 5-7 minutes more.
7. Serve it!

Nutrition value/serving: calories 380, fat 31.5, fiber 0.7, carbs 2.8, protein 22.1

Low Carb Morning Casserole

Prep time: 5 minutes , Cooking time: 10 minutes , Servings: 3

Ingredients:
- 3 oz cauliflower hash brown, cooked
- 3 eggs, whisked
- ¾ cup almond milk
- 2 oz chorizo, chopped
- 1 oz mozzarella, sliced
- 1/3 teaspoon chili flakes
- ½ teaspoon butter

Directions:
1. Melt the butter and whisk it together with the chili flakes, chorizo, almond milk, and eggs.
2. Add hash brown and stir gently.
3. Place the egg mixture in the cake pan and place in the Ninja Foodi.
4. Cook on Air Crisp 365 F for 8 minutes.
5. Then add sliced mozzarella on the top and cook for 2 minutes more, or until you get the desired doneness.
6. Enjoy!

Nutrition value/serving: calories 326, fat 28.2, fiber 1.9, carbs 5.8, protein 14.7

Western Omelet

Prep time: 5 minutes , Cooking time: 34 minutes , Servings: 2

Ingredients:
- 3 eggs, whisked
- 5 tablespoon almond milk
- 3 oz chorizo, chopped
- 1 green pepper, chopped
- ¼ teaspoon salt
- ¾ teaspoon chili flakes
- 1 oz Feta cheese, crumbled

Directions:
1. Mix up together all the ingredients and stir gently.
2. Pour the mixture into the omelet pan.
3. Preheat Ninja Foodi at "Roast/Bake" mode at 320 F for 4 minutes.
4. Then transfer the pan with an omelet in Ninja Foodi and cook at the same mode for 30 minutes.
5. Serve the cooked meal hot!

Nutrition value/serving: calories 424, fat 34.9, fiber 1.9, carbs 6.8, protein 21.9

Keto Cheddar Bites

Prep time: 6 minutes , Cooking time: 12 minutes , Servings: 4

Ingredients:
- 4 eggs
- ¼ cup heavy cream
- 3 oz Cheddar cheese, shredded
- 3 oz shrimps, peeled, cooked
- ½ teaspoon salt
- ½ cup of water

Directions:
1. Beat the eggs in the bowl and whisk well.
2. Add heavy cream, salt, and cheese. Stir it.
3. Chop the shrimps roughly and add in egg mixture.
4. Pour the egg mixture into the muffin molds.
5. Add water in the pot.
6. Place the muffins molds on the rack.
7. Cover the molds with the foil well.
8. Close the lid and seal it.
9. Cook the bites on High for 12 minutes. (Natural pressure release)
10. Discard the foil from bites and transfer them on the serving plates. Taste it!

Nutrition value/serving: calories 200, fat 14.6, fiber 0, carbs 1.1, protein 15.8

Bacon Jalapeno

Prep time: 6 minutes , Cooking time: 3 minutes , Servings: 3

Ingredients:
- 6 jalapeno peppers
- 1 teaspoon minced garlic
- 6 tablespoon cream cheese
- 6 bacon strips, chopped, cooked
- ½ teaspoon salt
- 1 oz ground beef, cooked
- ¼ teaspoon ground cumin

Directions:
1. Trim the ends of the peppers and remove all the seeds from inside.
2. Mix up together the minced garlic, cream cheese, salt, and ground cumin. Add the ground beef and stir well. Add bacon.
3. Fill the peppers with the mixture and transfer on the rack.
4. Lower the air fryer lid and cook the jalapenos for minutes at 365 F.
5. Serve the meal immediately!

Nutrition value/serving: calories 301, fat 26, fiber 1.2, carbs 3, protein 12.9

Eggs in Mushroom Hats

Prep time: 10 minutes , Cooking time: 9 minutes , Servings: 1

Ingredients:
- 4 oz mushroom hats
- 4 quail eggs
- ¼ teaspoon salt
- ½ teaspoon ground black pepper
- 1 teaspoon butter, melted

Directions:
1. Spread the mushroom hats with the butter inside.
2. Then beat the eggs into the mushroom hats and sprinkle with the ground black pepper and salt.
3. Transfer the mushroom hats on the rack and lower the air fryer lid.
4. Cook the meal at 365 F for 7 minutes.
5. Then check the mushrooms and cook them for 2 minutes more.
6. Serve it!

Nutrition value/serving: calories 118, fat 8.2, fiber 1., carbs 4.6, protein 8.4

Butter Chicken Bites

Prep time: 10 minutes , Cooking time: 11 minutes , Servings: 3

Ingredients:

- 10 oz chicken thighs, boneless, skinless
- 1 teaspoon turmeric
- 1 teaspoon chili flakes
- ½ teaspoon salt
- ¼ teaspoon ground nutmeg
- ¾ teaspoon ground ginger
- ½ cup heavy cream
- 2 tablespoon butter
- 1 teaspoon kosher salt

Directions:

1. Preheat Ninja Foodi pot at Saute/Stear mode for 5 minutes.
2. Toss the butter in the pot and melt it.
3. Add turmeric, chili flakes, salt, and ground nutmeg. Then, add ground ginger and salt.
4. Bring to boil the mixture.
5. Meanwhile, chop the chicken thighs roughly.
6. Transfer the chicken thighs in the pot and cooks for 5 minutes at Saute mode.
7. After this, add heavy cream and close the lid. Seal the lid.
8. Select Pressure mode and set High pressure
9. Cook it for 6 minutes. Then make a quick pressure release.
10. Chill the cooked chicken bites little and serve!

Nutrition value/serving: calories 322, fat 22.3, fiber 0.3, carbs 1.5, protein 28

Quiche Lorraine

Prep time: 10 minutes , Cooking time: 15 minutes , Servings: 4

Ingredients:

- 4 eggs, whisked
- ½ teaspoon salt
- ½ teaspoon cayenne pepper
- ¼ cup heavy cream
- 2 oz bacon, chopped
- 1 tablespoon butter
- 3oz Parmesan, grated
- ½ teaspoon dried basil

Directions:

1. Preheat Ninja Foodi at "Saute/Stear" mode for 5 minutes.
2. Then add butter and melt it.
3. Add bacon and saute it for 4 minutes.
4. Meanwhile, whisk together the eggs, salt, cayenne pepper, dried basil, and heavy cream.
5. When the bacon is cooked – add the egg mixture and lower the air fryer lid.
6. Cook the meal for 10 minutes at 365 F.
7. Then top the egg mixture with the grated cheese and cook for 5 minutes more.
8. Serve it!

Nutrition value/serving: calories 260, fat 20.5, fiber 0.1, carbs 1.6, protein 17.8

Breakfast Muffins

Prep time: 10 minutes , Cooking time: 15 minutes , Servings: 2

Ingredients:
- 1 tablespoon cream cheese
- 1 teaspoon butter
- 1 egg, beaten
- 1 tablespoon almond flour
- 2 oz Cheddar cheese, grated
- ¼ teaspoon ground black pepper
- ½ teaspoon salt
- ½ teaspoon paprika
- ½ cup water (for cooking on High)

Directions:
1. Mix up together the cream cheese, butter, egg, almond flour, cheese, ground black pepper, salt, and paprika.
2. Whisk the mixture until smooth.
3. After this, pour ½ cup of water in the pot. Insert the rack.
4. Transfer the batter in the prepared muffins molds and place on the rack.
5. Cover the muffins with the foil and close the lid.
6. Make sure you seal the lid and cook on PRESSURE mode (High) for 15 minutes.
7. Then make the quick pressure release for 5 minutes.
8. Chill the muffins little and serve!

Nutrition value/serving: calories 203, fat 17, fiber 0.7, carbs 1.9, protein 11.1

Chorizo Fritatta

Prep time: 10 minutes , Cooking time: 20 minutes , Servings: 6

Ingredients:
- 5 eggs, whisked
- 1 oz fresh parsley, chopped
- 3 oz chorizo, chopped
- 1 teaspoon salt
- ¼ green pepper, chopped
- 1 teaspoon butter
- ¼ cup heavy cream
- 1 oz broccoli, chopped
- 1 oz Cheddar cheese, grated
- 1 teaspoon cream cheese
- 1 teaspoon paprika
- 1 cup of water (for cooking on High pressure)

Directions:
1. Grease the springform pan with the butter.
2. Then place the layer of green pepper and broccoli.
3. After this, whisk together eggs, parsley, salt, heavy cream, cream cheese, and paprika.
4. Add chorizo and cheese. Stir gently and transfer the mixture in the pan. Flatten it gently.
5. Pour water in the pan and place the springform cake on the rack.
6. Close the lid and seal it.
7. Cook the meal on High (Pressure mode) for 20 minutes. Then use the quick pressure release method for 5 minutes.
8. Serve it!

Nutrition value/serving: calories 166, fat 13.4, fiber 0.5, carbs 1.8, protein 9.7

Asparagus Frittata

Prep time: 10 minutes , Cooking time: 21 minutes , Servings: 2

Ingredients:
- 2 oz asparagus, chopped
- 3 eggs, whisked
- 2 tablespoons almond milk
- 1 teaspoon almond flour
- ½ teaspoon salt
- ¼ teaspoon cayenne pepper
- ½ oz Parmesan, grated
- 1 teaspoon coconut oil

Directions:
1. Preheat the pot on "Saute/Stear mode.
2. Add coconut oil and chopped asparagus.
3. Saute the vegetable for 3 minutes.
4. Meanwhile, mix up together the almond milk, whisked, eggs, almond flour, cayenne pepper, and grated cheese.
5. Pour the egg mixture into the pot.
6. Close the lid and seal it.
7. Cook the frittata on High (Pressure mode) for 15 minutes.
8. After this, make a quick pressure release.
9. Lower the air fryer lid and cook the meal at 400 F for 6 minutes more.
10. When the surface of the frittata is crusty enough – finish cooking and serve it!

Nutrition value/serving: calories 165, fat 12.3, fiber 1.1, carbs 3.1, protein 11.8

Curry Shredded Chicken

Prep time: 10 minutes , Cooking time: 35 minutes , Servings: 2

Ingredients:
- 1-pound chicken breast, skinless, boneless
- 1 teaspoon curry paste
- 2 tablespoons butter
- 1 teaspoon cayenne pepper
- ½ cup of water

Directions:
1. Rub the chicken breast with the curry paste and place in the pot.
2. Sprinkle the poultry with cayenne pepper and add butter.
3. Pour water in the pot and close the lid. Seal the lid.
4. Set Pressure mode and cook on High for 30 minutes.
5. Then make natural pressure release for 10 minutes.
6. Open the lid and shred the chicken inside the pot with the help of the fork.
7. Then close the lid and saute the chicken for 5 minutes more.
8. Serve it!

Nutrition value/serving: calories 380, fat 18.8, fiber 0.2, carbs 1.2, protein 48.4

Classical Fried Eggs

Prep time: 5 minutes , Cooking time: 10 minutes , Servings: 2

Ingredients:
- 4 eggs
- 1 teaspoon butter
- ¼ teaspoon ground black pepper
- ¾ teaspoon salt

Directions:
1. Grease the small egg pan with the butter.
2. Beat the eggs in the egg pan and sprinkle with the ground black pepper and salt.
3. Transfer the egg pan in the pot and lower the air fryer lid.
4. Cook the eggs for 10 minutes at 350 F.
5. Serve the cooked eggs immediately!

Nutrition value/serving: calories 143, fat 10.7, fiber 0.1, carbs 0.9, protein 11.1

Eggs in Bacon Cups

Prep time: 10 minutes , Cooking time: 15 minutes , Servings: 4

Ingredients:
- 4 eggs
- 1 tablespoon butter
- 1 teaspoon dried parsley
- ¼ teaspoon cayenne pepper
- ¼ teaspoons paprika
- 4 bacon strips
- 1 oz Parmesan, grated

Directions:
1. Grease the small ramekins with butter.
2. Then secure the bacon strips on the edges of every ramekin.
3. Beat the egg in the center of every ramekin.
4. Sprinkle the eggs with paprika, dried parsley, cayenne pepper, and cheese.
5. Place the ramekins in the pot and lower the air fryer lid.
6. Cook the egg at 365 F for 15 minutes.
7. Chill the meal little and serve!

Nutrition value/serving: calories 212, fat 17.8, fiber 0.1, carbs 0.7, protein 11.9

Chicken Sandwiches

Prep time: 10 minutes , Cooking time: 15 minutes , Servings: 4

Ingredients:
- 1-pound chicken thighs, boneless, skinless
- 1 cup lettuce
- 1 teaspoon apple cider vinegar
- ½ teaspoon chili flakes
- 1 teaspoon red hot pepper
- ½ teaspoon turmeric
- 1 teaspoon white pepper
- ½ cup of water
- 1 tablespoon low-sodium soy sauce
- 1 tablespoon butter
- 1 oz Cheddar cheese, shredded

Directions:
1. Preheat Ninja Foodi at Saute/Stear mode for 5 minutes.
2. Toss the butter inside the pot.
3. Then rub the chicken thighs with the chili flakes, red hot pepper, turmeric, white pepper, and sprinkle with the soy sauce and apple cider vinegar.
4. Place the chicken in the pot and cook it for 5 minutes.
5. After this, close the lid and seal it.
6. Cook the chicken on High pressure for 5 minutes – quick pressure release).
7. After this, shred the chicken and remove ½ part of all the liquid from the form.
8. Lower the air fryer lid and cook the chicken at 400 F for 5 minutes more.
9. Transfer the cooked chicken on the lettuce leaves and sprinkle with cheese.
10. Taste it!

Nutrition value/serving: calories 276, fat 13.7, fiber 0.3, carbs 1.4, protein 35

Green Beans Omelet

Prep time: 7 minutes , Cooking time: 14 minutes , Servings: 2

Ingredients:
- 3 eggs, whisked
- 1 tablespoon cream cheese
- 1 oz green beans
- 1 teaspoon butter
- ¼ teaspoon salt
- ¼ teaspoon chili flakes

Directions:
1. Preheat Ninja Foodi on Saute/Stear mode.
2. Toss butter inside.
3. Add green beans and saute them for 4 minutes.
4. Meanwhile, whisk together the eggs and cream cheese.
5. Add salt and chili flakes. Stir the liquid.
6. Pour the liquid in the pot and stir gently with the help of a spatula.
7. Lower the air fryer lid and cook an omelet for 10 minutes at 360 F.
8. Serve it!

Nutrition value/serving: calories 133, fat 10.2, fiber 0.5, carbs 1.7, protein 9

Chili Chicken Bites

Prep time: 7 minutes , Cooking time: 25 minutes , Servings: 3

Ingredients:
- 12 oz chicken fillet
- 1 teaspoon chili flakes
- ½ teaspoon chili pepper
- ½ teaspoon red hot pepper
- ¼ teaspoon ground cumin
- ½ teaspoon salt
- 1 tablespoon butter
- ¾ cup heavy cream

Directions:
1. Cut the chicken fillet into the cubes.
2. Mix up together all the spices.
3. Combine together the chicken cubes and spices.
4. Then toss the butter in Ninja Foodi pot and melt it on Saute/Stear mode.
5. Place the chicken cubes in the pot and saute them for 5 minutes. Stir time to time.
6. After this, add cream and stir well.
7. Lower the air fryer lid and cook the chicken bites at 360 F for 20 minutes.
8. When the time is over – serve the chicken immediately!

Nutrition value/serving: calories 354, fat 23.4, fiber 0.1, carbs 1.1, protein 33.5

Breakfast Pork Chops

Prep time: 10 minutes , Cooking time: 30 minutes , Servings: 2

Ingredients:
- 2 pork chops
- 1 teaspoon butter
- ½ teaspoon dried cilantro
- 1 oz Mozzarella, sliced
- ½ teaspoon cayenne pepper
- ¾ cup of water

Directions:
1. Sprinkle the pork chops with the dried cilantro and cayenne pepper.
2. Toss the butter in Foodi and melt it on Saute/Stear mode.
3. Add pork chops and cook them for 2 minutes from each side.
4. Add water and close the lid.
5. Cook the meat on "Saute/Stear" mode for 25 minutes.
6. When the pork chops are cooked – open the lid and cover the meat with the sliced cheese.
7. Lower the air fryer lid and cook the meat for 3 minutes more at 400 F.
8. Enjoy!

Nutrition value/serving: calories 314, fat 24.4, fiber 0.1, carbs 0.8, protein 22.1

Asparagus and Bacon Plate

Prep time: 6 minutes , Cooking time: 9 minutes , Servings: 2

Ingredients:
- 2 oz bacon, chopped
- 4 oz asparagus, chopped
- ½ teaspoon salt
- ½ teaspoon ground black pepper
- 1 tablespoon butter
- 1 cup water, for cooking

Directions:
1. Place the bacon on the air fryer rack and sprinkle with the ground black pepper.
2. Lower the air fryer lid and cook the bacon at 400 F for 8 minutes.
3. Flip the bacon into another side after 4 minutes of cooking.
4. Then transfer the cooked bacon on the plate.
5. Pour water in the pot and insert steamer rack.
6. Place the asparagus and close the lid.
7. Cook the asparagus on High for 5 minutes. Then make quick pressure release.
8. Transfer the cooked asparagus over the bacon.
9. Add butter and salt.
10. Serve it!

Nutrition value/serving: calories 217, fat 17.7, fiber 1.3, carbs 3, protein 11.9

Jalapeno Chicken Wings

Prep time: 15 minutes , Cooking time: 15 minutes , Servings: 4

Ingredients:
- 12 oz chicken wings
- 2 jalapeno peppers, chopped
- 1 teaspoon minced garlic
- 1 tablespoon coconut oil
- ¼ cup of water
- 1 tablespoon butter
- ½ teaspoon salt

Directions:
1. Blend together the jalapeno peppers and minced garlic until smooth.
2. Then combine together the pepper mixture, salt, and coconut oil.
3. Brush every chicken wing with the pepper mixture and let for 10 minutes to marinate.
4. Place the marinated chicken wings in the pot. Add butter and water.
5. Close the lid and seal it.
6. Cook the chicken wings for 10 minutes on High 9Pressure mode).
7. Then make a quick pressure release.
8. Lower the air fryer lid and cook the chicken wings for 5 minutes more at 400 F.
9. Serve!

Nutrition value/serving: calories 220, fat 12.7, fiber 0.3, carbs 0.8, protein 24.8

Hard Boiled Eggs with Bacon Filling

Prep time: 10 minutes , Cooking time: 15 minutes , Servings: 2

Ingredients:
- 4 eggs
- 1 teaspoon cream cheese
- 1 oz bacon, chopped, cooked
- 1/2 teaspoon minced garlic

Directions:
1. Place the eggs in the air fryer basket and lower the air fryer lid.
2. Cook the eggs at 250 F for 15 minutes.
3. Meanwhile, mix up together the cooked bacon, minced garlic, and cream cheese.
4. When the eggs are cooked – chill them in ice water and peel.
5. Cut the eggs into the halves and transfer the egg yolks in the cream cheese mixture.
6. Stir it carefully until homogenous.
7. Fill the egg whites with the filling and serve!

Nutrition value/serving: calories 205, fat 15.3, fiber 0, carbs 1.2, protein 16.5

Lunch Recipes

Enchilada Soup

Prep time: 10 minutes , Cooking time: 15 minutes , Servings: 4

Ingredients:

- 1 cup coconut milk, full-fat
- 1 tablespoon almond flour
- ¾ cup chicken stock
- ½ teaspoon salt
- ½ teaspoon ground cumin
- ½ teaspoon ground white pepper
- ¼ teaspoon chili flakes
- ½ teaspoon smoked paprika
- ½ white onion, diced
- ¼ tomato, chopped
- 14 oz chicken breast, skinless, boneless

Directions:

1. Take the saucepan and combine together coconut milk and almond flour.
2. Whisk the mixture and add chicken stock, salt, ground cumin, ground white pepper, chili flakes, smoked paprika, and stir well.
3. Preheat the liquid on the medium-high heat until boils.
4. After this, place the chicken breast, tomato, and onion in the Ninja Foodi.
5. Add prepared coconut milk liquid and close the lid.
6. Seal the lid and cook on High for 11 minutes.
7. Then make a quick pressure release and transform the chicken breast on the plate.
8. Shred the chicken breast with the help of the fork and return in the pot.
9. Stir well and serve!

Nutrition value/serving: calories 271, fat 17.8, fiber 2, carbs 5.7, protein 23.1

Aromatic Meatballs

Prep time: 8 minutes , Cooking time: 11 minutes , Servings: 4

Ingredients:

- 2 cups ground beef
- 1 teaspoon Taco seasoning
- 1 tablespoon sugar-free marinara sauce
- ½ teaspoon salt
- 1 egg, beaten
- 1 tablespoon minced garlic

Directions:

1. Place all the ingredients in the big mixing bowl.
2. Combine together all the ingredients with the help of the spoon or fingertips.
3. After this, make the small size meatballs and put them in a layer in the air fryer rack.
4. Lower the air fryer lid and cook the meatballs for 11 minutes at 355 F.
5. Serve the meatballs immediately!

Nutrition value/serving: calories 205, fat 12.4, fiber 0.1, carbs 2.2, protein 19.7

Classic Pot Roast

Prep time: 10 minutes , Cooking time: 1 hour 20 minutes , Servings: 2

Ingredients:
- 1 carrot, chopped
- 1 cup beef broth
- 12 oz chuck roast, boneless, chopped
- 1 bay leaf
- 1 teaspoon salt
- ½ onion
- 1 garlic clove, crushed
- ½ teaspoon ground black pepper
- 1 teaspoon peppercorns
- 1 tablespoon almond flour

Directions:
1. Sprinkle the chuck roast with the salt, ground black pepper, and put in the preheated for 5 minutes put (Saute/Stea) mode.
2. Cook the meat for 4 minutes. Stir it from time to time.
3. After this, add beef broth, chopped carrot, bay leaf, salt, onion, crushed garlic, almond flour, and peppercorns.
4. Close the lid and seal it.
5. Cook the meal on High (Pressure mode) for 55 minutes.
6. When the time is over – make the natural pressure release for 25 minutes.
7. Serve it!

Nutrition value/serving: calories 434, fat 16.5, fiber 2, carbs 7.9, protein 60

Keto Ramen

Prep time: 7 minutes , Cooking time: 34 minutes , Servings: 4

Ingredients:
- 3 oz Konjac noodles
- 1-pound chicken breast, skinless, boneless
- 1 teaspoon ground black pepper
- 1 teaspoon salt
- 4 cup of water
- 1 teaspoon garlic powder
- 1 teaspoon Erythritol
- 1 tablespoon low-sodium soy sauce
- ½ white onion, diced
- 1 teaspoon mustard seeds

Directions:
1. Place the chicken breast, ground black pepper, salt, water, garlic powder, Erythritol, and diced onion in the pot.
2. Add mustard seeds and close the lid. Seal the lid.
3. Then cook the mixture on High (Pressure mode) for 25 minutes.
4. Then make a quick pressure release.
5. Open the lid and transfer the chicken breast on the plate. Shred it and return back in the pot.
6. Add low-sodium soy sauce and Konjac noodles.
7. Close and seal the lid and cook the meal ob High for 4 minutes more.
8. Then make natural pressure release for 5 minutes.
9. Serve it!

Nutrition value/serving: calories 146, fat 3.1, fiber 1.3, carbs 4.5, protein 24.8

Paprika Lamb Shanks

Prep time: 15 minutes , Cooking time: 60 minutes , Servings: 6

Ingredients:
- 2 packs lamb shanks
- 1 tablespoon dried paprika
- 1 tablespoon smoked paprika
- 1 carrot, chopped
- 1 teaspoon onion powder
- 1 teaspoon salt
- 1 teaspoon white pepper
- 2 cup of water
- 1 tablespoon butter

Directions:
1. Set Sear/Saute mode and add butter, smoked paprika, and paprika.
2. Cook on High for 1 minute.
3. Add the lamb shank and sear the meat until it is light brown (appx. 3-4 minutes).
4. Add onion powder, salt, white pepper, and water and close the lid. Seal it.
5. Cook on High for 20 minutes.
6. When the time is over – make a quick pressure release and open the lid.
7. Add chopped carrot and stir the meal.
8. Close and seal the lid and keep cooking on High for 14 minutes more.
9. After this, make the quick pressure release for 5 minutes.
10. Set "broil" mode and cook the meal for 8 minutes more.
11. Enjoy!

Nutrition value/serving: calories 287, fat 13.7, fiber 4.7, carbs 11.6, protein 28

Keto Italian Style Beef

Prep time: 15 minutes , Cooking time: 40 minutes , Servings: 3

Ingredients:
- 1-pound beef roast, boneless
- 1 tablespoon Italian style seasoning
- ½ teaspoon kosher salt
- 1 tablespoon butter, softened
- 1 garlic clove, crushed
- 1 teaspoon dried rosemary
- 1 teaspoon coconut oil
- ½ cup chicken stock
- 1 jalapeno pepper, sliced

Directions:
1. Preheat Ninja Foodi on Saute/Stear mode for 5 minutes.
2. Add coconut oil, crushed garlic clove, and dried rosemary.
3. Saute the mixture for 1 minute.
4. Meanwhile, rub the beef roast with the Italian style seasoning and salt.
5. Place the beef roast in the pot and saute it for 5 minutes.
6. Then flip the meat into another side and saute for 3 minutes more.
7. Add butter and chicken stock.
8. Close the lid and seal it.
9. Press Pressure bottom and set the High pressure.
10. Cook the meat for 25 minutes. Then make quick pressure release.
11. Add sliced jalapeno pepper and transfer the meat on Air fryer rack.

12. Transfer the cooked liquid in the bowl and keep it warm – this is the sauce.
13. Lower the air fryer lid and cook the meat for 15 minutes at 390 F.
14. Place the cooked meat in the bowl with warm sauce and serve!

Nutrition value/serving: calories 360, fat 15.6, fiber 0.3, carbs 1.3, protein 50.2

Juicy Chicken Marsala

Prep time: 10 minutes , Cooking time: 15 minutes , Servings: 3

Ingredients:
- 1-pound chicken breast, skinless, boneless
- 1/3 cup heavy cream
- ¾ cup almond milk
- 1 teaspoon salt
- 1/3 white onion, diced
- 1 tablespoon butter
- 1 teaspoon turmeric
- ½ teaspoon ground black pepper
- ¼ teaspoon minced garlic
- 1 teaspoon dried dill
- 1 tablespoon almond flour

Directions:
1. Preheat the pot on Saute/Stear mode for 5 minutes.
2. Meanwhile, mix up together the salt, turmeric, ground black pepper, minced garlic, dried dill, and stir it carefully.
3. Chop the chicken breast roughly.
4. Mix up together the spices and chicken breast.
5. Toss the butter in the preheated pot and add chicken.
6. Saute the poultry for 5 minutes. Stir it from time to time.
7. After this, add almond milk and heavy cream. Stir it.
8. Close the lid and seal it.
9. Cook the meal on High (pressure mode) for 7 minutes.
10. Then make a quick pressure release.
11. Open the lid and add almond flour. Stir the meal very carefully.
12. Cook the meal on Saute/Stear mode for 2 minutes more.
13. Stir the meal and transfer into the serving dishes. Enjoy!

Nutrition value/serving: calories 412, fat 28, fiber 2.1, carbs 6.2, protein 34.5

Chicken Soup

Prep time: 5 minutes , Cooking time: 10 minutes , Servings: 2

Ingredients:
- 1 oz celery, diced
- 1 cup chicken stock
- 6 oz chicken fillet
- 1 teaspoon dried dill
- 1/3 carrot, diced
- ½ teaspoon salt
- 1/3 teaspoon ground black pepper
- ½ teaspoon onion powder

Directions:
1. Chop the chicken fillet into small cubes and place in the pot.
2. Add onion powder, ground black pepper, and salt.
3. Close the lid and seal it.
4. Cook the chicken on Pressure mode (High pressure) for 6 minutes.
5. After this, make a quick pressure release and open the lid.
6. Add diced carrot, celery, and dried dill. Close the lid and seal it.
7. Cook on High for 4 minutes more.
8. When the time is over – make the quick pressure release for 5 minutes.
9. Ladle the soup into bowls and serve!

Nutrition value/serving: calories 177, fat 6.6, fiber 0.7, carbs 2.8, protein 25.3

Keto Pizza Casserole

Prep time: 15 minutes , Cooking time: 25 minutes , Servings: 4

Ingredients:
- 1 tomato, sliced
- 3 oz chorizo, sliced
- 2 tablespoons butter
- 1 cup ground turkey
- ½ teaspoon ground black pepper
- 1 teaspoon smoked paprika
- 3 oz Cheddar cheese, shredded
- 1 oz mozzarella, sliced
- ½ teaspoon dried basil
- ½ teaspoon dried oregano
- ½ teaspoon ground thyme
- ½ cup chicken stock

Directions:
1. Preheat Ninja Foodi on Saute/Stear mode for 5 minutes.
2. Toss butter and melt it.
3. Add the ground turkey and saute it for 5 minutes.
4. Then sprinkle turkey with the ground black pepper and smoked paprika. Stir it well and add sliced chorizo. Place it in the layer.
5. After this, add the layer of Cheddar cheese. Sprinkle the meal with dried basil and oregano.
6. After this, add the layer of mozzarella.
7. Sprinkle the cheese with ground thyme.
8. Pour the chicken stock and close the lid.
9. Seal it and cook on High (Pressure mode) for 15 minutes.
10. Then make natural pressure release for 10 minutes.
11. Lower the Air fryer lid and cook the pizza for 10 minutes more at 400 F.

12. When you get the crunchy surface – the casserole is cooked.
13. Enjoy!

Nutrition value/serving: calories 261, fat 22.4, fiber 0.6, carbs 2.3, protein 12.9

Cauliflower Soup

Prep time: 10 minutes , Cooking time: 10 minutes , Servings: 5

Ingredients:
- 1 cup heavy cream
- 1 cup chicken stock
- 3 tablespoons cream cheese
- 2 oz Cheddar cheese, shredded
- 1 cup of water
- 1-pound cauliflower head
- 1 teaspoon minced garlic
- ½ teaspoon dried dill
- 2 oz bacon, chopped, cooked

Directions:
1. Preheat Ninja Foodi on Saute/Stear mode for 5 minutes.
2. Chop the cauliflower into the small pieces and place in the preheated pot.
3. Add heavy cream, chicken stock, water, minced garlic, and dried dill.
4. Close the lid and seal it.
5. Cook the mixture on High (Pressure mode) for 5 minutes.
6. Then make quick pressure release for 5 minutes.
7. Transfer the cauliflower mixture in the blender and blend until smooth.
8. After this, ladle the hot soup in the bowl.
9. Top every bowl with Cheddar cheese and chopped bacon.
10. Serve it!

Nutrition value/serving: calories 237, fat 19.7, fiber 2.3, carbs 6.4, protein 10

Low Carb Chili

Prep time: 15 minutes , Cooking time: 20 minutes , Servings: 6

Ingredients:
- 1-pound ground chicken
- 1-pound ground beef
- 1 teaspoon minced garlic
- 1 tomato, chopped
- 1 cup chicken stock
- ½ teaspoon cumin
- ½ teaspoon dried oregano
- ½ teaspoon white pepper
- ¼ teaspoon thyme
- 1 teaspoon onion powder
- ¼ cup heavy cream
- 2 tablespoon butter

Directions:
1. Mix up together the minced garlic, chopped tomato, cumin, dried oregano, white pepper, thyme, and onion powder.
2. Combine together all the ground meat and spice mixture.
3. Stir it well with the help of the spoon.
4. Transfer the meat mixture in the pot.
5. Add cream, butter, and chicken stock.
6. Close the lid and seal it.
7. Cook it on High pressure for 15 minutes.
8. After this, allow the natural pressure release for 10 minutes.
9. Lower the air fryer lid and cook the chili for 10 minutes more at 400 F.
10. Serve the cooked meal hot!

Nutrition value/serving: calories 326, fat 14.3, fiber 0.3, carbs 1.5, protein 45.3

Marinara Beef Ribs

Prep time: 10 minutes , Cooking time: 25 minutes , Servings: 6

Ingredients:
- 2-pound short beef ribs
- 3 tablespoons keto marinara sauce
- 1 teaspoon onion powder
- ½ teaspoon garlic powder
- 1 teaspoon chili flakes
- ½ cup beef broth
- 1 teaspoon butter
- ¼ teaspoon cayenne pepper

Directions:
1. Rub the ribs with the onion powder, chili flakes, and cayenne pepper.
2. Place the butter and beef ribs in Ninja Foodi pot and start to cook them on Saute/Stear mode.
3. Flip the ribs into another side after 5 minutes of cooking.
4. Add beef broth and close the lid.
5. Select Pressure mode (high pressure) and seal the lid.
6. Cook the beef ribs for 15 minutes.
7. Then make a quick pressure release and remove the liquid from the pot.
8. Brush the ribs with the marinara sauce and lower the air fryer lid.
9. Cook the ribs at 400 F for 10 minutes more.
10. Serve the cooked ribs hot!

Nutrition value/serving: calories 604, fat 55.8, fiber 0.2, carbs 1.3, protein 21.9

Keto Chicken Nuggets

Prep time: 10 minutes , Cooking time: 9 minutes , Servings: 5

Ingredients:
- 1-pound chicken fillet
- 3 eggs, whisked
- 2 tablespoon almond flour
- 1 teaspoon turmeric
- ¼ teaspoon ground black pepper
- 1 tablespoon coconut oil

Directions:
1. Cut the chicken fillet into the medium size pieces.
2. Then mix up together the almond flour, turmeric, and ground black pepper.
3. Place the chicken pieces into the bowl and add whisked egg.
4. Stir the poultry carefully.
5. Then dip every chicken piece in the turmeric mixture.
6. Sprinkle Foodi basket with the coconut oil and place the chicken nuggets inside.
7. Lower the air fryer lid and cook the chicken nuggets for 6 minutes at 400 F;
8. Then flip the chicken nuggets into another side and cook for 3 minutes more.
9. Serve the nuggets and enjoy!

Nutrition value/serving: calories 251, fat 13.5, fiber 0.4, carbs 1.2, protein 30.2

Fragrant Sardines

Prep time: 10 minutes , Cooking time: 8 minutes , Servings: 2

Ingredients:
- 8 oz sardines, peeled
- ¼ cup almond flour
- 1 teaspoon salt
- 1 teaspoon paprika
- 1 teaspoon turmeric
- 1 tablespoon olive oil

Directions:
1. Mix up together the almond flour, paprika, turmeric, an salt.
2. Coat the sardines into the almond flour mixture.
3. Place the sardines in the springform pan and place it on the trivet of Ninja Foodi. Sprinkle with the olive oil.
4. Lower the air fryer lid and set Air Crisp mode.
5. Cook the fish for 4 minutes at 400 F.
6. Then turn the fish into another side and cook for 4 minutes more.
7. Enjoy!

Nutrition value/serving: calories 108, fat 10.2, fiber 1, carbs 2.1, protein 3.8

Salmon Cakes

Prep time: 10 minutes , Cooking time: 10 minutes , Servings: 2

Ingredients:
- 8 oz salmon fillet
- ½ cup spinach
- ½ teaspoon salt
- 1 tablespoon coconut flakes
- 1 tablespoon almond flour
- ½ teaspoon ground paprika
- 1 teaspoon coconut oil
- 1 egg, whisked

Directions:
1. Blend the spinach in the blender until it is smooth.
2. Then discard the liquid and leave only greens.
3. Combine together the blended spinach, egg, ground paprika, and salt. Stir well.
4. Then chop the salmon into the tiny pieces and add in the spinach.
5. Stir until homogenous.
6. Make the medium salmon cakes.
7. Combine together the almond flour and coconut flakes.
8. Sprinkle the salmon cakes with the almond flour mixture from both sides.
9. Sprinkle Foodi basket with the coconut oil and place salmon cakes in one layer.
10. Lower the air fryer lid and cook the salmon cakes at 400 F for 5 minutes from each side. For crunchy crust – cook cakes 3 minutes extra.
11. Serve the cooked salmon cakes immediately.

Nutrition value/serving: calories 234, fat 14.1, fiber 1, carbs 1.9, protein 25.9

Duck Patties

Prep time: 10 minutes , Cooking time: 10 minutes , Servings: 2

Ingredients:
- 7 oz duck breast, skinless, boneless
- ¼ teaspoon salt
- 1 tablespoon almond flour
- 1 teaspoon turmeric
- 1 teaspoon butter
- ¼ teaspoon cayenne pepper
- 1 egg white

Directions:
1. Chop the duck breast and transfer into the blender.
2. Blend the poultry until smooth.
3. Then transfer the blended duck breast in the bowl.
4. Add salt, turmeric, cayenne pepper, and egg white.
5. Mix up the mixture with the help of spoon until homogenous.
6. Then make the medium patties from the poultry mixture and cover patties in the almond flour.
7. Preheat Ninja Foodi on "saute/Stear" mode.
8. Toss the butter in the basket.
9. When the butter is melted – add the duck patties.
10. Cook the meal for 3 minutes from each side.
11. After this, lower the air fryer lid and cook the meal at 400 F for 3 minutes from each side or until you get the desired crust of the meal.
12. Serve the duck patties immediately!

Nutrition value/serving: calories 238, fat 13.1, fiber 1.8, carbs 4, protein 26.8

Asparagus Soup

Prep time: 8 minutes , Cooking time: 12 minutes , Servings: 2

Ingredients:
- 1 cup chicken stock
- 3 tablespoons heavy cream
- 5 oz asparagus
- 1 teaspoon paprika
- ½ teaspoon salt
- 1 oz Cheddar cheese, grated
- 1 teaspoon butter
- 1 cup water, for cooking

Directions:
1. Pour water in Ninja Foodi and insert rack.
2. Place the asparagus on the rack and close the lid.
3. Cook the asparagus on Pressure mode (High pressure) for 5 minutes.
4. Then make quick pressure release and transfer the asparagus in the blender. Blend it.
5. Remove all liquid from the pot.
6. Place chicken stock inside.
7. Add butter, salt, paprika, and heavy cream.
8. Set Saute/Stear mode and cook the liquid for 5-6 minutes or until the butter is melted and the liquid starts to boil.
9. Then add the blended asparagus and stir well.
10. Transfer the cooked soup into the bowls and top with the grated cheese.
11. Enjoy!

Nutrition value/serving: calories 174, fat 15.5, fiber 1.9, carbs 4.5, protein 6.1

Nutritious Bacon Salad

Prep time: 10 minutes , Cooking time: 7 minutes , Servings: 3

Ingredients:
- 1 cup broccoli florets
- 3 oz bacon, chopped
- 1 tablespoon butter, melted
- 1 tablespoon olive oil
- ½ teaspoon minced garlic
- ½ teaspoon paprika
- 1 tablespoon pumpkin seeds
- 3 tablespoon heavy cream
- 1 oz Parmesan, grated
- 1 cup water, for cooking

Directions:
1. Pour water in Ninja Foodi and insert rack.
2. Place the broccoli florets on the rack and close the lid.
3. Select PRESSURE mode and set High pressure. Close and seal the lid.
4. Cook the broccoli for 5 minutes and then make a quick pressure release.
5. Then remove all the liquid from the pot and transfer the broccoli on the chopping board.
6. Place the bacon on the rack and lower the air fryer mode.
7. Cook the bacon for 5 minutes at 400 F.
8. Then stir the bacon and cook it for 1 minute more. Increase the time of cooking if you want crunchy bacon.
9. After this, chop the broccoli roughly and place it the salad bowl.
10. Add cooked bacon, melted butter, olive oil, minced garlic, pumpkin seeds, heavy cream, and stir well.
11. Sprinkle the salad with grated cheese and serve immediately!

Nutrition value/serving: calories 337, fat 29.4, fiber 1, carbs 4.1, protein 15.5

Taco Meat

Prep time: 15 minutes , Cooking time: 27 minutes , Servings: 4

Ingredients:
- 1.5-pound chicken breast, skinless, boneless
- 1 tablespoon taco seasoning
- 1 teaspoon minced garlic
- 1 teaspoon salt
- 1 tablespoon butter
- ¼ cup heavy cream
- ¼ cup chicken stock
- 1 tablespoon fresh cilantro, chopped

Directions:
1. Chop the chicken breast into the medium cubes.
2. Place the chicken in the pot and sprinkle with taco seasoning.
3. Add minced garlic, salt, butter, cream, chicken stock, and stir gently.
4. Close the lid and seal it.
5. Cook the meat on PRESSURE mode (High pressure) for 27 minutes.
6. Then make the quick pressure release for 10 minutes.
7. Transfer the meal in the bowl and serve!

Nutrition value/serving: calories 254, fat 10, fiber 0.3, carbs 1.6, protein 36.3

Keto Minestrone Soup

Prep time: 15 minutes , Cooking time: 13 minutes , Servings: 2

Ingredients:
- 2 cups chicken stock
- ½ cup ground beef
- 1 white onion, diced
- 1 teaspoon salt
- ½ teaspoon cayenne pepper
- 2 oz celery stalk, chopped
- 1 teaspoon lemon juice
- ¼ cup spinach, chopped
- ½ cup of water
- ½ teaspoon dried basil
- ¼ teaspoon dried oregano

Directions:
1. Mix up together the ground beef and all spices.
2. Toss the mixture in Ninja Foodi and saute on Saute/Stear mode for 3 minutes. Stir it from time to time.
3. Then add diced onion, celery stalk, and spinach.
4. Add water and saute it for 5 minutes more.
5. After this, add the chicken stock and close the lid.
6. Select PRESSURE mode and cook on High for 3 minutes.
7. Make the quick pressure release for 5 minutes and let the soup rest for 10 minutes more.
8. Serve it!

Nutrition value/serving: calories 105, fat 4.9, fiber 1.9, carbs 7.3, protein 8.2

Bacon-Avocado Mash

Prep time: 10 minutes , Cooking time: 5 minutes , Servings: 2

Ingredients:
- 2 avocado, peeled, cored or 1 cup avocado, pureed
- 2 oz bacon, sliced
- ½ teaspoon salt
- 1 teaspoon butter, melted
- 1 teaspoon heavy cream
- ½ teaspoon cayenne pepper
- ½ teaspoon smoked paprika
- 1 teaspoon olive oil
- ½ teaspoon minced garlic

Directions:
1. Make the puree from avocado.
2. Place the sliced bacon on the rack in the pot and lower the air fryer lid.
3. Cook the bacon for 5 minutes at 400 F.
4. Meanwhile, whisk together the melted butter, heavy cream, olive oil, cayenne pepper, minced garlic, and smoked paprika.
5. When the bacon is cooked – chill it little and chop.
6. Mix up together the avocado puree and bacon.
7. Add butter mixture and churn well.
8. Serve the meal warm!

Nutrition value/serving: calories 341, fat 28.7 fiber 6.8, carbs 10.3, protein 13.3

Kofta Kebabs

Prep time: 10 minutes , Cooking time: 25 minutes , Servings: 2

Ingredients:
- 10 oz ground lamb
- 1 teaspoon chili flakes
- 1 teaspoon onion powder
- ½ teaspoon ground thyme
- ½ teaspoon salt
- 1 teaspoon olive oil

Directions:
1. Combine together the ground lamb, chili flakes, onion powder, ground thyme, and salt.
2. Stir the mixture.
3. Take the bamboo sticks and skewer the meat into them to make the kebabs.
4. Place the kebabs on the trivet of Ninja Foodi and lower the air fryer lid.
5. Cook the meat on Air Crisp mode for 15 minutes at 380 F.
6. Then check the meat and cook it for 10 minutes more.
7. Serve the cooked meat immediately!

Nutrition value/serving: calories 289, fat 12.8, fiber 0.2, carbs 1.2, protein 40

Fish Salad

Prep time: 10 minutes , Cooking time: 5 minutes , Servings: 2

Ingredients:
- 1-pound cod fillet, skinless, boneless
- 1 teaspoon ground black pepper
- 1 teaspoon salt
- 1 tablespoon lemon juice
- 1 tablespoon olive oil
- ½ teaspoon chili flakes
- 1 cup lettuce, chopped
- 1 cup water, for cooking

Directions:
1. Rub the cod fillet with the ground black pepper and salt and place on the trivet of Ninja Foodi.
2. Our water in the pot and insert the trivet with fish.
3. Close the lid and cook the fish on High pressure (Pressure mode) for 5 minutes. Then make a quick pressure release.
4. Meanwhile, place the chopped lettuce in the bowl.
5. Sprinkle it with the olive oil and stir.
6. When the fish is cooked – chop it roughly and add in the lettuce bowl.
7. Sprinkle the fish with the lemon juice and serve immediately!

Nutrition value/serving: calories 251, fat 1.1, fiber 0.5, carbs 1.7, protein 40.8

Mozzarella Duck Breast

Prep time: 10 minutes , Cooking time: 25 minutes , Servings: 2

Ingredients:
- 1-pound duck breast, skinless, boneless
- ½ cup chicken stock
- 1 tablespoon fresh cilantro
- 1 teaspoon butter
- 1 teaspoon ground black pepper
- 1 teaspoon salt
- 1 teaspoon heavy cream
- 3 oz Mozzarella, sliced

Directions:
1. Make the cut in the duck breast and fill it with the fresh cilantro and sliced Mozzarella.
2. Then rub the duck breast with the ground black pepper, salt, heavy cream, and place in the pot.
3. Add butter and set Saute/Stear mode.
4. Cook the duck breast for 5 minutes from each side.
5. After this, add chicken stock and lower the air fryer lid.
6. Cook the meal on Air Crisp mode for 20 minutes at 370 F.
7. When the duck breast is cooked – serve it with the remaining chicken stock from the pot.
8. Enjoy!

Nutrition value/serving: calories 443, fat 19.6, fiber 0.3, carbs 2.5, protein 62.3

Egg Salad

Prep time: 5 minutes , Cooking time: 15 minutes , Servings: 2

Ingredients:
- 3 eggs
- ½ white onion, sliced
- 1 teaspoon olive oil
- 1 avocado, chopped
- 3 tablespoons heavy cream
- ½ teaspoon salt
- ½ teaspoon paprika

Directions:
1. Place the eggs on the trivet and insert it in Ninja Foodi.
2. Lower the air fryer lid and cook the eggs at 270 F for 15 minutes.
3. Meanwhile, combine together the onion, chopped avocado, heavy cream, salt, and paprika.
4. When the eggs are cooked – chill them in icy water and peel.
5. Cut the eggs into the quarters and add in the avocado mixture.
6. Stir the salad and serve!

Nutrition value/serving: calories 410, fat 36.9, fiber 7.5, carbs 12.7, protein 11.1

Side Dishes

Crispy Kale

Prep time: 5 minutes , Cooking time: 10 minutes , Servings: 4

Ingredients:
- 1 teaspoon yeast
- 2 cups Kale, Italian dark-leaf
- ½ teaspoon chili flakes
- ¼ teaspoon salt
- 2 tablespoons coconut oil

Directions:
1. Tear the kale roughly and place in the bowl.
2. Sprinkle the kale with the salt, coconut oil, yeast, and chili flakes.
3. Mix up the kale well until homogenous.
4. Insert the air fryer basket and in the Ninja Foodi and transfer the kale.
5. Air fryer the meal for 10 minutes or until you get the desired crisps.
6. Serve!

Nutrition value/serving: calories 78, fat 6.9, fiber 0.7, carbs 3.9, protein 11.4

Keto Jalapeno Poppers

Prep time: 10 minutes , Cooking time: 9 minutes , Servings: 4

Ingredients:
- 4 bacon strips
- 8 jalapeno peppers
- ¼ cup cream cheese
- 2 oz Parmesan, shredded

Directions:
1. Remove the seeds from jalapeno peppers.
2. Mix up together the cream cheese and shredded Parmesan.
3. Then fill the jalapeno peppers with cheese mixture.
4. Wrap every jalapeno pepper in a ½ bacon strip.
5. Place the jalapeno peppers on the rack and lower the air fryer lid.
6. Cook the meal for 9 minutes at 360 F.
7. Serve the jalapeno peppers hot!

Nutrition value/serving: calories 208, fat 17.5, fiber 1.1, carbs 3, protein 10

Tender Asparagus Bites

Prep time: 10 minutes , Cooking time: 9 minutes , Servings: 4

Ingredients:
- 14 oz asparagus, stalks
- 4 oz prosciutto, sliced
- ½ teaspoon dried red hot pepper

Directions:
1. Sprinkle asparagus with the dried red hot pepper and wrap every stalk in prosciutto.
2. Place the asparagus in the rack and lower the air fryer lid.
3. Cook the meal for 3 minutes at 365 F.
4. Serve it warm!

Nutrition value/serving: calories 81, fat 2.3, fiber 2.8, carbs 5.8, protein 10.8

Cauliflower Fries

Prep time: 10 minutes , Cooking time: 9 minutes , Servings: 4

Ingredients:
- 1/3 cup water
- 13 oz cauliflower
- 1 tablespoon butter
- 1 teaspoon minced garlic
- ½ teaspoon minced onion
- ½ teaspoon ground black pepper
- ½ teaspoon salt
- 2 oz Parmesan, grated

Directions:
1. Pour water in Ninja Foodi pot.
2. Then cut the cauliflower into the medium florets.
3. Place the cauliflower florets in the pot and close the lid.
4. Seal the lid and cook on Low for 3 minutes.
5. Meanwhile, churn together the butter, minced garlic, minced onion, ground black pepper, and salt.
6. When the mass is homogenous – add Parmesan and stir it with the help o the spoon well.
7. When the time is over and cauliflower florets are cooked, remove the pressure lid; brush cauliflower generously with the butter mixture.
8. Lower the air fryer lid and cook it at 400 F for 15 minutes.
9. Then shake the fried well and cook more if you don't get the desired crispness.
10. Taste it!

Nutrition value/serving: calories 81, fat 2.3, fiber 2.8, carbs 5.8, protein 10.8

Stuffed Mushrooms

Prep time: 10 minutes , Cooking time: 6 minutes , Servings: 3

Ingredients:
- 10 oz mushroom hats
- 1 oz fresh parsley, chopped
- 2 oz Parmesan, grated
- 1 oz Cheddar cheese, grated
- 2 tablespoon cream cheese
- ½ teaspoon chili flakes
- ½ teaspoon dried oregano

Directions:
1. Combine together the chopped parsley, all grated cheese, cream cheese, chili flakes, and dried oregano.
2. Then fill the mushroom hats with the cheese mixture well.
3. Place the mushroom hats on the rack and lower the Air fryer lid.
4. Cook the meal at 400 F for 6 minutes. Check if the mushrooms are cooked – and cook them for 2-3 minutes more if desired.
5. Serve!

Nutrition value/serving: calories 147, fat 9.9, fiber 1.4, carbs 4.9, protein 12.2

Crispy Okra

Prep time: 10 minutes , Cooking time: 20 minutes , Servings: 3

Ingredients:
- 1 tablespoon yeast
- 13 oz okra
- 1 tablespoon coconut oil
- ½ teaspoon salt
- ½ teaspoon white pepper

Directions:
1. Mix up together the coconut oil and yeast.
2. Add salt and whisk pepper and whisk the mixture.
3. Trim the okra and sprinkle it with the yeast mixture well.
4. Preheat Ninja Foodi at Air crisp mode (400F – 5 minutes).
5. Then place the okra in the rack and lower the air fryer lid.
6. Crisp the vegetables for 20 minutes at 400 F.
7. Shake the vegetables after 15 minutes of cooking.
8. Check if the okra is crispy enough and transfer it on the serving plates or cook for 5 minutes more.

Nutrition value/serving: calories 101, fat 5, fiber 4.9, carbs 10.9, protein 3.9

Cauliflower Steaks

Prep time: 10 minutes , Cooking time: 30 minutes , Servings: 4

Ingredients:
- 1-pound cauliflower head
- 1 teaspoon salt
- 2 tablespoon coconut oil
- 1 teaspoon chili flakes
- 1 teaspoon dried basil
- ½ teaspoon ground nutmeg

Directions:
1. Preheat Ninja Foodi at "Saute/Sear" mode for 5 minutes (High pressure).
2. Cut the cauliflower head into the steaks.
3. Sprinkle steaks with the salt, chili flakes, dried basil, and ground nutmeg.
4. Pour 1 tablespoon of coconut oil in the pot and add cauliflower steaks.
5. Sear the cauliflower steaks for 8 minutes, flip it into another side from time to time.
6. Make the same steps with all remaining steaks.
7. After this, sprinkle the cooked steaks with the remaining coconut oil and place on the rack.
8. Lower the air fryer lid and roast the steaks at 365 F for 10 minutes or until you get the desired crispness.
9. Serve the cauliflower steaks warm!

Nutrition value/serving: calories 89, fat 7, fiber 2.9, carbs 6.2, protein 2.3

Parmesan Broccoli

Prep time: 8 minutes , Cooking time: 8 minutes , Servings: 4

Ingredients:
- 15 oz broccoli florets
- 1 teaspoon salt
- 1 oz Parmesan, grated
- 1 teaspoon ground coriander
- 2 cups heavy cream
- 1 teaspoon garlic powder

Directions:
1. Wash the broccoli florets carefully.
2. Pour the water in the pot (follow the directions of Ninja Foodi) and insert the rack.
3. Sprinkle the broccoli with the salt, ground coriander, and garlic powder.
4. Place the broccoli on the rack. Close the lid.
5. Set "Steam" mode and cook the broccoli for 8 minutes.
6. Meanwhile, boil the heavy cream – it should be hot.
7. When the broccoli is cooked – transfer it on the serving plates, sprinkle with the hot heavy cream and grated cheese.
8. Enjoy!

Nutrition value/serving: calories 151, fat 7.4, fiber 2.8, carbs 8.2, protein 5.7

Keto Mashed "Potato"

Prep time: 7 minutes , Cooking time: 5 minutes , Servings: 4

Ingredients:
- 1-pound cauliflower florets
- 2 tablespoons butter
- 1 teaspoon salt
- 1 teaspoon dried basil
- 1 cup water (for cooking)

Directions:
1. Pour water in Ninja Foodi pot and insert rack.
2. Place the cauliflower florets on the rack and close the lid.
3. Seal the lid and select Pressure. Cook the cauliflower on High for 5 minutes.
4. After the time is over, use the quick pressure release.
5. Transfer the cauliflower florets in the blender and blend until smooth.
6. Add the butter in the hot mashed cauliflower.
7. Stir it and add 2-3 tablespoons of water from the pot if the mashed cauliflower is not fluffy enough.
8. Sprinkle the cauliflower with the dried basil and salt and stir well.
9. Serve it hot!

Nutrition value/serving: calories 79, fat 5.9, fiber 2.8, carbs 6, protein 2.3

Zucchini "Noodles"

Prep time: 5 minutes , Cooking time: 2 minutes , Servings: 4

Ingredients:
- 2 zucchini
- 1 oz Parmesan, grated
- ¼ cup chicken stock
- ½ teaspoon salt
- 1 teaspoon lemon juice

Directions:
1. Wash the zucchini carefully and make the noodles with the help of spiralizer.
2. After this, place the zucchini noodles in the pot. Add salt and chicken stock.
3. Close the lid and seal it.
4. Cook the side dish on High (Pressure mode) for 2 minutes.
5. Then make quick pressure release.
6. Strain the noodles and transfer on the plates.
7. Sprinkle the noodles with the lemon juice and grated cheese.
8. Serve it immediately!

Nutrition value/serving: calories 39, fat 1.8, fiber 1.1, carbs 3.6, protein 3.5

Keto Spaghetti Squash

Prep time: 8 minutes , Cooking time: 10 minutes , Servings: 4

Ingredients:
- 1 teaspoon butter
- 1-pound spaghetti squash
- 1 teaspoon smoked paprika
- 1 cup water (for cooking)

Directions:
1. Cut the spaghetti squash into the halves.
2. Remove all the seeds and add butter in every half.
3. Sprinkle the vegetable with the smoked paprika.
4. Pour water in the pot and insert rack.
5. Place the spaghetti squash on the rack (of the squash is too big – chop it).
6. Close the lid and seal it.
7. Cook the vegetable for 10 minutes on High.
8. After this, make the quick pressure release for 5 minutes.
9. Remove the squash from the pot and shred it with the help of the fork.
10. Discard the skin and transfer the shredded vegetables on the serving plates.
11. Taste it!

Nutrition value/serving: calories 32, fat 2.1, fiber 0.9, carbs 2.6, protein 0.7

Creamy Spinach

Prep time: 5 minutes , Cooking time: 10 minutes , Servings: 4

Ingredients:
- 3 cups spinach, chopped
- 1 cup cream
- 1 teaspoon butter, melted
- ½ teaspoon salt
- ½ teaspoon ground black pepper

Directions:
1. Mix up together the chopped spinach, cream, melted butter, salt, and ground black pepper.
2. Stir the spinach gently and transfer in the cake form. Flatten it gently.
3. Place the spinach in Foodi and lower the air fryer lid.
4. Cook the side dish for 5 minutes at 365 F.
5. Then open the lid and stir the spinach well.
6. Cook it for 5 minutes more at 365 F.
7. Serve it!

Nutrition value/serving: calories 53, fat 44, fiber 0.6, carbs 2.9, protein 1.2

Bok Choy with Mushrooms

Prep time: 7 minutes , Cooking time: 7 minutes , Servings: 3

Ingredients:
- 10 oz bok choy, chopped
- 5 oz white mushrooms, chopped
- 1 teaspoon salt
- 1 tablespoon coconut oil

Directions:
1. Combine together bok choy and mushrooms.
2. Mix up the ingredients and sprinkle with the salt and coconut oil.
3. Make a shake to the ingredients and transfer them in Ninja Foodi.
4. Lower the air fryer lid and cook the side dish for 7 minutes at 400 F.
5. Stir the cooked meal gently and serve it!

Nutrition value/serving: calories 61, fat 4.9, fiber 1.4, carbs 3.6, protein 2.9

Herbed Chicken Drumsticks

Prep time: 8 minutes , Cooking time: 18 minutes , Servings: 3

Ingredients:
- 14 oz chicken drumsticks
- 1 teaspoon dried thyme
- 1 teaspoon dried oregano
- ½ teaspoon dried rosemary
- ½ teaspoon chili flakes
- 1 teaspoon salt
- 1 teaspoon almond flour
- 1 teaspoon cayenne pepper
- 1 tablespoon coconut oil
- 1 teaspoon dried cilantro
- 1 teaspoon onion powder
- 1 teaspoon garlic powder

Directions:
1. Mix up together all the spices and almond flour.
2. Then dip the chicken drumsticks in the spice mixture.
3. Sprinkle Foodi basket with the coconut oil,
4. Place the chicken drumsticks in the basket in one layer.
5. Lower the air fryer lid and cook the chicken for 10 minutes at 365 F.
6. When the time is over – open the lid and flip the drumsticks into another side.
7. Cook the chicken for 8 minutes more.
8. Serve the cooked chicken drumsticks immediately!

Nutrition value/serving: calories 278, fat 12.7, fiber 0.8, carbs 2.5, protein 36.9

Aromatic Brussel Sprouts

Prep time: 5 minutes , Cooking time: 10 minutes , Servings: 4

Ingredients:

- 1 teaspoon minced garlic
- 1-pound Brussel sprouts
- 1 tablespoon butter, melted
- ½ teaspoon salt

Directions:

1. Churn together the minced garlic, butter, and salt.
2. Then mix up together the butter mixture and Brussel sprouts.
3. Place the vegetables in Ninja Foodi basket and lower the air fryer lid.
4. Cook the vegetables for 10 minutes at 385 F.
5. When Brussel sprouts are cooked – stir them gently and serve!

Nutrition value/serving: calories 75, fat 3.3, fiber 4.3, carbs 10.5, protein 3.9

Cauliflower Rice

Prep time: 6 minutes , Cooking time: 6 minutes , Servings: 4

Ingredients:

- 1-pound cauliflower head, shredded
- 1 tablespoon butter
- 1 oz green beans
- ½ teaspoon salt
- 1 cup water, for cooking

Directions:

1. Pour water in Ninja Foodi basket.
2. Place the shredded cauliflower and green beans in the springform pan and place in the basket.
3. Close the lid and seal it.
4. Set the Pressure mode (High pressure) and cook the cauliflower rice for 3 minutes.
5. Then make a quick pressure release.
6. Remove water from the basket.
7. Add butter and salt in the cauliflower rice and stir it.
8. Lower the air fryer lid and cook the cauliflower rice for 3 minutes at 365 F.
9. Enjoy the cooked meal!

Nutrition value/serving: calories 56, fat 3, fiber 3.1, carbs 6.5, protein 2.4

Hummus

Prep time: 10 minutes , Cooking time: 6 minutes , Servings: 6

Ingredients:

- 1-pound cauliflower head
- 1 cup chicken stock
- 1 teaspoon chili flakes
- 1 teaspoon tahini sauce
- 3 tablespoons coconut oil
- 1 teaspoon salt

Directions:

1. Chop the cauliflower head roughly and place in Ninja Foodi.
2. Add chicken stock and close the lid. Seal it.
3. Select PRESSURE mode and put on High. Cook the cauliflower for 6 minutes.
4. Then make a quick pressure release and transfer the cauliflower without liquid in the blender and blend until smooth.
5. Add coconut oil, salt, tahini sauce, and chili flakes.
6. Pulse the mixture 2-3 times more.
7. Transfer the cooked hummus into the bowl and serve!

Nutrition value/serving: calories 82, fat 7.2, fiber 1.9, carbs 4.2, protein 1.7

Turmeric Cauliflower Head

Prep time: 10 minutes , Cooking time: 15 minutes , Servings: 4

Ingredients:

- 1 oz fresh parsley, chopped
- 10pound cauliflower head
- 1 tablespoon turmeric
- 1 teaspoon salt
- ¼ cup almond milk
- 1 teaspoon butter, melted
- 1 cup water, for cooking

Directions:

1. Wash the cauliflower head carefully.
2. Pour water in Ninja Foodi and add cauliflower head.
3. Select Pressure mode (low pressure) and cook the vegetable for 3 minutes.
4. After this, remove all the liquid from the pot and transfer the cauliflower head in the bowl.
5. Whisk together the turmeric, salt, almond milk, and melted butter.
6. Brush the cauliflower head with the turmeric mixture generously.
7. Then place the cauliflower head on the rack.
8. Lower the air fryer lid and select Air Crisp mode.
9. Cook the cauliflower for 12 minutes or until you get the crunchy surface.
10. Sprinkle the cooked cauliflower with the parsley and serve!

Nutrition value/serving: calories 56, fat 1.3, fiber 4.2, carbs 10, protein 3.3

Keto Cauliflower Couscous

Prep time: 10 minutes , Cooking time: 13 minutes , Servings: 4

Ingredients:
- 1 oz almonds, chopped
- 1-pound cauliflower head, shredded
- 1 teaspoon olive oil
- 1 teaspoon salt
- ½ teaspoon curry powder
- ½ green pepper
- 1 tablespoon butter

Directions:
1. Chop the green pepper in the same pieces as cauliflower.
2. Then insert the rack in Ninja Foodi.
3. Place the layer of green pepper in the springform pan, after this add the layer of the chopped cauliflower and sprinkle the vegetables with the olive oil.
4. Place the springform pan in Foodi and lower the air fryer lid.
5. Set Air Crisp mode 380 F and cook the vegetables for 6 minutes.
6. After this, stir the vegetables and cook for 7 minutes more or until you get the light brown color.
7. When the vegetables are cooked – transfer them in the bowl and add salt. Chopped almonds, curry powder, and butter.
8. Stir the couscous until homogenous.
9. Serve it!

Nutrition value/serving: calories 109, fat 7.8, fiber 4.1, carbs 8.4, protein 3.9

Zucchini Sticks

Prep time: 10 minutes , Cooking time: 6 minutes , Servings: 4

Ingredients:
- 2 zucchini
- 1 oz Parmesan, grated
- 1 egg, whisked
- 1 tablespoon almond flour
- ½ teaspoon cayenne pepper
- 1 teaspoon paprika
- 1 oz bacon, sliced

Directions:
1. Cut zucchini into the sticks.
2. Mix up together the whisked egg, salt, cayenne pepper, and paprika.
3. Dip the zucchini sticks in the whisked egg mixture.
4. Then mix up together the almond flour and grated parmesan.
5. Coat the zucchini into the cheese mixture and wrap into the bacon slices.
6. Place the zucchini sticks on the trivet of Ninja Foodi.
7. Lower the air fryer mode and select Air Crisp.
8. Cook the zucchini sticks at 400 F for 6 minutes.
9. Serve the side dish hot!

Nutrition value/serving: calories 135, fat 9.4, fiber 2.1, carbs 5.6, protein 9.1

Hot Jalapeno Hash

Prep time: 5 minutes , Cooking time: 10 minutes , Servings: 4

Ingredients:
- 4 jalapeno peppers, chopped
- 6 oz zucchini, chopped
- ½ cup chicken stock
- 1 teaspoon butter
- 3 oz bacon, chopped, cooked
- 1 teaspoon ground black pepper

Directions:
1. Place the zucchini and jalapeno peppers in the pot of Ninja Foodi.
2. Add butter, bacon, ground black pepper, and chicken stock.
3. Close the lid and set PRESSURE (High). Cook the meal for 5 minutes.
4. Then make the natural pressure release for 10 minutes.
5. Chill the cooked meal well and serve with the remaining gravy (chicken stock).

Nutrition value/serving: calories 139, fat 10.2, fiber 1.2, carbs 3.2, protein 8.7

Green Bean Salad

Prep time: 5 minutes , Cooking time: 14 minutes , Servings: 3

Ingredients:
- 8 oz green beans
- 2 tablespoons butter
- 5 oz celery, sliced
- 1 tablespoon pecans, chopped
- ½ teaspoon salt
- 1 teaspoon cayenne pepper
- 1 tablespoon olive oil
- ½ teaspoon minced garlic
- 1 cup water, for cooking

Directions:
1. Pour water in Ninja Foodi and insert the trivet.
2. Place the green beans and sliced fennel on the trivet.
3. Close the lid and cook at Pressure mode (High pressure) for 8 minutes.
4. Then make a quick pressure release.
5. Remove the liquid from the pot and place the vegetables inside it.
6. Add butter, cayenne pepper, minced garlic, and olive oil.
7. Set Saute/Stear mode and cook the vegetables for 6 minutes. Stir them well.
8. When the vegetables are cooked – transfer them in the bowls and sprinkle with pecans.
9. Enjoy the meal warm!

Nutrition value/serving: calories 236, fat 11.4, fiber 5.6, carbs 11.4, protein 3.2

Cauliflower Tortilla

Prep time: 10 minutes , Cooking time: 9 minutes , Servings: 4

Ingredients:
- 11 oz cauliflower, chopped
- 1 teaspoon salt
- ½ teaspoon dried basil
- ½ teaspoon dried dill
- 2 egg, whisked
- 1 cup water, for cooking

Directions:
1. Pour water in Ninja Foodi.
2. Add cauliflower and close the lid. Seal the lid.
3. Cook the cauliflower on Pressure mode (High pressure) for 3 minutes.
4. Then make a quick pressure release.
5. Transfer the cauliflower in the blender and remove the liquid from the pot.
6. Blend the cauliflower until smooth.
7. Then mix up together the whisked eggs, dried dill, basil, salt, and stir well until you get the lemon-sticky dough.
8. Make the medium tortillas from the mixture and place them on the trivet in Ninja Foodi.
9. Lower the air fryer lid and cook the tortillas for 6 minutes at 400 F.
10. Chill the cooked tortillas and serve!

Nutrition value/serving: calories 51, fat 2.3, fiber 2, carbs 4.4, protein 4.3

Fried Keto Pickles

Prep time: 10 minutes , Cooking time: 7 minutes , Servings: 4

Ingredients:
- 7 oz pickles, sliced
- 1 egg, whisked
- 2 tablespoons heavy cream
- 2 tablespoons almond flour
- 1 teaspoon paprika

Directions:
1. Mix up together the almond flour and paprika.
2. Dip the sliced pickles in the whisked egg and them coat in almond flour mixture.
3. Place the pickles on the trivet of Ninja Foodi and lower the air fryer lid.
4. Cook the side dish for 7 minutes at 400 F.
5. When the pickles are cooked – chill them well and serve!

Nutrition value/serving: calories 70, fat 5.7, fiber 1.2, carbs 2.5, protein 2.5

Creamy Eggplants

Prep time: 15 minutes , Cooking time: 15 minutes , Servings: 5

Ingredients:
- 2 eggplants, chopped, peeled
- 1 teaspoon minced garlic
- ½ cup heavy cream
- 1 teaspoon ground black pepper
- 1 teaspoon salt
- 1 tablespoon fresh dill, chopped
- 1 tablespoon butter

Directions:
1. Sprinkle the eggplants with ground black pepper, salt, and minced garlic.
2. Stir well and let the vegetables for 10 minutes to marinate.
3. Meanwhile, preheat Ninja Foodi at Saute/Stear mode for 5 minutes at 365 F.
4. Toss the butter in the preheated pot and melt it.
5. Add the chopped eggplants and saute them for 5 minutes.
6. After this, add heavy cream and lower the pressure cooker lid.
7. Set Pressure mode (High pressure) for 5 minutes (370 F).
8. When the time is over – make a quick pressure release.
9. Then lower the air fryer lid and cook the eggplants at 400 F for 5 minutes.
10. Serve the cooked side dish immediately!

Nutrition value/serving: calories 120, fat 7.2, fiber 7.9, carbs 14, protein 2.6

Main Dishes

Barbecue Ribs

Prep time: 10 minutes , Cooking time: 30 minutes , Servings: 7

Ingredients:

- 2.5-pound pork ribs
- 1 teaspoon apple cider vinegar
- ¼ cup of water
- 1 tablespoon butter
- 1 garlic clove, crushed
- 1 teaspoon Italian seasoning
- 1 tomato, chopped

Directions:

1. Combine together apple cider vinegar, water. Butter, Italian seasoning, and crushed garlic.
2. Add tomato and transfer the liquid in the pot.
3. Place the pork ribs in the pot and close the lid. Seal the lid.
4. Cook the ribs on High for 20 minutes. After this, make a quick pressure release.
5. Remove the pressure lid and cook the ribs on Air Crisp mode for 10 minutes more at 400 F.
6. When you get the desired crispness – the meal is cooked.
7. Taste it!

Nutrition value/serving: calories 461, fat 30.6, fiber 0.1, carbs 0.6, protein 43

Keto Burgers

Prep time: 10 minutes , Cooking time: 12 minutes , Servings: 2

Ingredients:

- 10 oz ground chuck
- 1 teaspoon Italian seasoning
- 1 teaspoon salt
- 1 teaspoon ground black pepper
- 1 teaspoon minced garlic
- 1 cup lettuce

Directions:

1. Combine together the ground chuck, Italian seasoning, salt, ground black pepper, and minced garlic.
2. Make the medium burgers and place them on the rack
3. Lower the Air fryer lid and cook the burgers at 360 F for 10 minutes.
4. Then flip the meat onto another side and cook for 2 minutes more.
5. Garnish the cooked burgers with the lettuce and serve!

Nutrition value/serving: calories 404, fat 25.3, fiber 0.5, carbs 2.2, protein 39.4

Aromatic Chicken Wings

Prep time: 8 minutes , Cooking time: 25 minutes , Servings: 2

Ingredients:

- 1 teaspoon minced garlic
- 1 teaspoon minced onion
- ½ teaspoon salt
- ½ teaspoon white pepper
- 1 teaspoon ground cumin
- ½ teaspoon dried oregano
- 3 tablespoon almond milk
- 1 teaspoon almond flour
- 8 oz chicken wings, boneless

Directions:

1. Make the sauce for the wings: combine together the minced garlic and onion, salt, white pepper, ground cumin, dried oregano, almond milk, and almond flour.
2. Whisk the mixture well.
3. Then place the chicken wings on the rack and brush well with the sauce.
4. Lower the air fryer lid and cook the wings for 20 minutes at 365 F.
5. Then check the wings and flip them into another side.
6. Brush another side of the chicken wings with the remaining sauce and cook for 5 minutes more.
7. Serve!

Nutrition value/serving: calories 356, fat 21.1, fiber 2.5, carbs 5.9, protein 36.7

Cauliflower Gratin

Prep time: 7 minutes , Cooking time: 22 minutes , Servings: 3

Ingredients:

- 1 cup heavy cream
- 1 egg, whisked
- 10 oz cauliflower florets, chopped
- 1 teaspoon salt
- ½ teaspoon ground black pepper
- ½ teaspoon turmeric
- 2 tablespoons almond milk
- 1 teaspoon butter
- 1 oz Cheddar cheese, shredded
- ½ cup of water

Directions:

1. Pour water in the pot.
2. Add cauliflower florets, salt, ground black pepper, turmeric, and butter.
3. Close the lid and seal it.
4. Cook on High for 3 minutes.
5. Meanwhile, mix up together Cheddar cheese and almond flour.
6. When the time is over – make a quick pressure release, add heavy cream and set "Saute" mode (Medium).
7. When the meal starts to boil, press "STOP".
8. Lower the air fryer lid and crisp the meal for 15 minutes at 400 F.
9. Enjoy!

Nutrition value/serving: calories 257, fat 23.2, fiber 2.8, carbs 7.4, protein 7.2

Piri Piri Crunchy Chicken Drumsticks

Prep time: 15 minutes , Cooking time: 18 minutes , Servings: 2

Ingredients:
- 8 drumsticks, skinless
- 1 tablespoon piri piri sauce
- 1 teaspoon dried rosemary
- 1 tablespoon butter
- ½ cup of water
- 1 teaspoon salt
- 1 teaspoon dried cumin
- ¼ teaspoon ground nutmeg
- ½ teaspoon hot chili pepper
- 1 teaspoon dried dill

Directions:
1. Rub the chicken drumsticks with the dried rosemary, salt, cumin, nutmeg, hot chili pepper, and dill.
2. Preheat Ninja Foodi on saute mode for 5 minutes (365F).
3. Then add the chicken drumsticks and water.
4. Add butter and close the lid. Seal it.
5. Cook the chicken on High (Pressure mode) for 10 minutes.
6. After this, make the quick pressure release for 5 minutes.
7. Put the chicken drumsticks on Air Crisp rack, add piri piri sauce, and lower the air fryer lid.
8. Cook the drumsticks for 8 minutes at 395 F or until you get the desired crispness.
9. Serve!

Nutrition value/serving: calories 224, fat 12.8, fiber 0.8, carbs 4.6, protein 27.7

Fragrant Mussels

Prep time: 10 minutes , Cooking time: 4 minutes , Servings: 6

Ingredients:
- 2-pound mussels
- 1 teaspoon garlic powder
- ½ onion, diced
- 1 teaspoon ground black pepper
- 1 teaspoon dried oregano
- 2 tablespoons butter
- ¼ cup heavy cream
- 1 teaspoon lemon juice

Directions:
1. Preheat the pot on Saute/Sear for 5 minutes at 365 F.
2. Add all the ingredients in the pot and close the lid.
3. Seal the lid and cook on Pressure mode (Low) 4 minutes.
4. When the time of cooking is finished – make a quick pressure release.
5. Transfer the cooked meal into the bowls and serve!

Nutrition value/serving: calories 188, fat 9.1, fiber 0.5, carbs 7.3, protein 18.4

Whole Chicken

Prep time: 15 minutes , Cooking time: 45 minutes , Servings: 10

Ingredients:
- 4-pound whole chicken
- ½ cup heavy cream
- 1 teaspoon onion powder
- ½ teaspoon ground cinnamon
- 1 teaspoon salt
- 1 teaspoon lemon zest
- 1 cup of water
- 1 teaspoon chili pepper
- 1 tablespoon smoked paprika
- 1 teaspoon hot pepper
- ½ teaspoon cayenne pepper
- 3 tablespoons butter

Directions:
1. Mix up together onion powder, ground cinnamon, salt, chile pepper, smoked paprika, hot pepper, cayenne pepper, and stir gently.
2. Then rub the chicken with the spice mixture.
3. After this, place lemon zest inside the chicken.
4. Leave the chicken for at least 1 hour to marinate.
5. After this, place the chicken in Foodi pot and add water.
6. Close the lid and seal it.
7. Press the bottom "PRESSURE" and cook on High for 20 minutes.
8. After this, make the quick pressure release for 10 minutes.
9. Remove the liquid from pot and place the chicken on air fryer rack.
10. Lower the air fryer lid and set Air Crisp mode.
11. Cook the chicken for 15 minutes at 400 F.
12. When the time is over – spread the hot chicken with butter and serve!

Nutrition value/serving: calories 400, fat 19.2, fiber 0.4, carbs 1.1, protein 52.8

Keto Paella

Prep time: 5 minutes , Cooking time: 23 minutes , Servings: 4

Ingredients:
- 10 oz cauliflower, shredded
- 1 teaspoon salt
- ½ teaspoon ground black pepper
- ½ teaspoon turmeric
- 1 teaspoon ground cumin
- 1 garlic clove, crushed
- ½ teaspoon ground nutmeg
- 1 teaspoon butter
- 8 oz mussels
- 8 oz shrimps, peeled
- 1 cup chicken stock
- 1 teaspoon cayenne pepper
- 1 teaspoon dried oregano
- ½ cup of water
- 8 oz chicken breast, boneless, skinless, chopped
- 1 tablespoon butter
- 1 tablespoon fresh parsley, chopped

Directions:
1. Set the "Saute/Sear" (High) and preheat the pot for 5 minutes.

2. Place butter, chicken breast, mussels, and shrimps in the pot.
3. Saute the ingredients for 5 minutes.
4. Add salt, ground black pepper, turmeric, ground cumin, crushed garlic, ground nutmeg, chicken stock, cayenne pepper, dried oregano, and water. Stir carefully.
5. Close the lid and seal it.
6. Select "Pressure" (HIGH) and cook the meal for 3 minutes.
7. Allow the natural pressure release for 10 minutes.
8. Enjoy the meal with the fresh parsley on the top!

Nutrition value/serving: calories 244, fat 8.1, fiber 2.4, carbs 8.4, protein 33.6

Aromatic Brisket

Prep time: 15 minutes , Cooking time: 57 minutes , Servings: 4

Ingredients:
- 2-pound beef brisket
- 1 cup chicken stock
- 1 teaspoon dried rosemary
- 1 teaspoon peppercorn
- 1 teaspoon thyme
- 1 teaspoon oregano
- 1 teaspoon salt
- 1 teaspoon garlic powder
- 1 tomato, chopped
- 5 oz celery stalk, chopped
- 1 tablespoon butter

Directions:
1. Rub the beef brisket with the dried rosemary, thyme, oregano, salt, and garlic powder.
2. Leave the meat for 10 minutes to marinate.
3. Meanwhile, preheat Ninja Foodi at "Saute/Stir" mode for 5 minutes.
4. Then toss the butter in the pot and melt it.
5. Place the beef brisket in the pot and saute it for 5 minutes from each side.
6. After this, add chicken stock, tomato, and celery stalk. Stir the ingredients.
7. Close the lid and seal it.
8. Cook the meat on Pressure mode (High) for 35 minutes.
9. After this, make a quick pressure release.
10. Remove the liquid from the pot and transfer it in the bowl (don't let it chill).
11. Insert the rack in the pot. Place the brisket on the rack.
12. Lower the air fryer lid and crisp the meat for 17 minutes at 400 F.
13. When the meat is cooked – transfer it into the serving bowl. Cut it into servings and sprinkle with the remaining liquid from the bowl.
14. Serve it!

Nutrition value/serving: calories 464, fat 17.4, fiber 1.4, carbs 3.3, protein 69.6

Pork Chops in Mushroom Sauce

Prep time: 15 minutes , Cooking time: 40 minutes , Servings: 5

Ingredients:
- 2-pound pork loin chops
- 2 oz white mushrooms, chopped
- 1 cup heavy cream
- ¼ cup beef broth
- 1 tablespoon butter
- 1 teaspoon salt
- 1 teaspoon cayenne pepper
- 1 teaspoon minced garlic
- ½ teaspoon ground thyme

Directions:
1. Mix up together the minced garlic, cayenne pepper, and salt.
2. Then rub the pork chops with the spice mixture.
3. Preheat the pot on "Saute/Stear" mode for 5 minutes.
4. Place the pork chops in the pot and cook them for 5 minutes from each side.
5. After this, mix up together the beef broth, heavy cream, and white mushrooms.
6. Pour the liquid in the pot and close the lid.
7. Seal the lid and choose Pressure mode.
8. Cook the meat on High 30 minutes.
9. After this, make the quick pressure release for 5 minutes.
10. Transfer the meal on the plates and serve!

Nutrition value/serving: calories 476, fat 26.1, fiber 0.3, carbs 1.5, protein 55.9

Jamaican Pork

Prep time: 15 minutes , Cooking time: 5 hours , Servings: 6

Ingredients:
- 2-pound pork shoulder, boneless
- 1 tablespoon jerk seasoning
- 1 teaspoon taco seasoning
- 1/3 cup chicken stock
- 1 teaspoon butter

Directions:
1. Rub the pork shoulder with the jerk seasoning and taco seasoning.
2. Then preheat Ninja Foodi at Saute/Stear mode for 5 minutes.
3. Toss the butter inside and melt it.
4. After this, add the pork shoulder and cook it for 10 minutes. Flip it into another side in half-way.
5. Then add chicken stock and close the lid.
6. Seal it and cook on Pressure mode (Low pressure) for 5 hours.
7. When the time is over – shred the meat and sprinkle with the remaining liquid.
8. Serve it!

Nutrition value/serving: calories 449, fat 33, fiber 0, carbs 0.4, protein 35.3

Cheesy Lasagna

Prep time: 10 minutes , Cooking time: 15 minutes , Servings: 5

Ingredients:

- 4 oz Mozzarella, sliced
- 2 tomatoes, chopped
- 2 cups ground beef
- 1 teaspoon ground black pepper
- ½ teaspoon salt
- 2 oz Parmesan, grated
- 1 teaspoon minced garlic
- ½ teaspoon paprika
- ½ teaspoon onion powder
- 2 tablespoons butter
- ¼ cup chicken stock
- 1 cup of water

Directions:

1. Preheat Ninja Foodi on Saute/Stear mode for 5 minutes.
2. Place the ground beef inside.
3. Add ground black pepper, salt, minced garlic, paprika, and onion powder.
4. Saute the ground meat for 7 minutes. Stir it from time to time.
5. After this, remove the ground meat from the pot.
6. Grease the non-sticky cakepan with the butter generously.
7. Then make the layer of the ground beef inside it.
8. Place the layer of Mozzarella.
9. After this, make the layer of the chopped tomatoes and Parmesan.
10. Repeat the steps until you finish all the ingredients. Bear in mind that the last layer should be cheese layer.
11. Pour chicken stock.
12. Pour water in the pot and place the lasagna.
13. Wrap lasagna in the foil and close the lid.
14. Seal the lid.
15. Cook the lasagna on High (Pressure mode) for 10 minutes.
16. After this, remove water from the pot and lower the air fryer lid.
17. Make the crunchy crust at 400 F for 5 minutes.
18. Chill the lasagna little and serve!

Nutrition value/serving: calories 257, fat 17.8, fiber 0.8, carbs 3.9, protein 21.1

Shrimps in Parmesan

Prep time: 8 minutes , Cooking time: 10 minutes , Servings: 3

Ingredients:

- 1-pound shrimps, peeled
- ¼ teaspoon garlic powder
- ½ teaspoon onion powder
- ½ teaspoon dried oregano
- 1 oz Parmesan, grated
- ½ teaspoon smoked paprika
- 1 cup water, for cooking

Directions:

1. Pour water in Ninja Foodi basket and insert trivet.
2. Place the shrimps on a trivet and close the lid.
3. Seal the lid and cook on Pressure mode (high) for 3 minutes. After this, make quick pressure release.

4. Meanwhile. Mix up together the garlic powder, onion powder, dried oregano, grated cheese, and smoked paprika.
5. Coat the cooked shrimps in the cheese mixture.
6. Place the shrimps in the empty basket and lower the air fryer lid.
7. Cook the shrimps for 7 minutes at 365 F.
8. When the shrimps are cooked – they will be crispy.
9. Enjoy!

Nutrition value/serving: calories 214, fat 4.7, fiber 0.3, carbs 3.5, protein 37.6

Steak Nuggets

Prep time: 10 minutes , Cooking time: 25 minutes , Servings: 4

Ingredients:
- 11 oz beef steak
- 1 egg, whisked
- 1 teaspoon salt
- ¼ teaspoon ground black pepper
- ¼ cup almond flour
- 1 teaspoon coconut oil

Directions:
1. Cut the beef steak into the cubes.
2. Sprinkle the meat with the salt and ground black pepper from each side.
3. Then dip the meat nuggets in the whisked egg.
4. Coat the meat nuggets in the almond flour.
5. Sprinkle Ninja Foodi basket with the coconut oil and place the meat nuggets inside in one layer.
6. Lower the air fryer lid and cook the nuggets for 15 minutes at 365 F.
7. Then flip the nuggets into another side and cook for 10 minutes more at 380 F.
8. When the time is over and the Nuggets are tender – transfer them in the bowl and serve with Keto dip.

Nutrition value/serving: calories 213, fat 10.4, fiber 0.8, carbs 1.7, protein 26.5

Lobster Tail

Prep time: 5 minutes , Cooking time: 4 minutes , Servings: 2

Ingredients:
- 12 oz lobster tails
- 2 tablespoons lemon juice
- 3 tablespoons butter, melted
- 1 teaspoon dried dill
- 1 cup water, for cooking

Directions:
1. Pour water in Ninja Foodi basket.
2. Then insert trivet.
3. Place the lobster tails on the trivet and close the pressure cooker lid.
4. Cook the tails on High for 4 minutes.
5. Then make a quick pressure release.
6. Meanwhile, whisk the melted butter with the lemon juice and dried dill – the dip is cooked.
7. Transfer the cooked lobster tails on the plate and serve with the butter dip.
8. Enjoy!

Nutrition value/serving: calories 310, fat 18.8, fiber 0.1, carbs 0.6, protein 32.7

Garlic Mackerel

Prep time: 10 minutes , Cooking time: 16 minutes , Servings: 4

Ingredients:
- 1.5-pound mackerel fillet
- 1 teaspoon minced garlic
- 1 teaspoon ground white pepper
- ½ teaspoon ground nutmeg
- 1 teaspoon butter
- ½ teaspoon salt
- ½ teaspoon dried rosemary
- 1 cup water, for cooking

Directions:
1. Rub the mackerel fillet with the dried rosemary. Warp the fish in the foil.
2. Pour water in Ninja Foodi basket and insert trivet.
3. Place mackerel on the trivet and close the lid.
4. Seal the lid and set Pressure mode (High).
5. Cook the fish for 6 minutes.
6. Meanwhile, make the sauce: mix up together the butter, minced garlic, ground white pepper, and ground nutmeg.
7. Churn the mixture.
8. When the fish is cooked – make a quick pressure release.
9. Discard the foil from the fish.
10. Clean the basket and place the sauce inside.
11. Add the fish and select "Saute/Stear" mode.
12. Cook the fish for 10 minutes more.
13. Serve it!

Nutrition value/serving: calories 458, fat 31.4, fiber 0.3, carbs 0.8, protein 40.7

Curry Chicken Breast

Prep time: 10 minutes , Cooking time: 35 minutes , Servings: 2

Ingredients:
- 1-pound chicken breast
- 1 tablespoon curry paste
- 2 tablespoons butter
- ½ cup heavy cream
- 1 teaspoon salt

Directions:
1. Rub the chicken with the curry paste.
2. Place the chicken breast in Ninja Foodi basket.
3. Add salt, cream, and butter.Select Saute/Stear mode and cook the chicken for 35 minutes.
4. When the time is over – transfer the chicken breast on the serving plate and slice.
5. Pour the remaining heavy cream sauce from the pot over the chicken breast!
6. Serve it!

Nutrition value/serving: calories 514, fat 32.7, fiber 0, carbs 3, protein 49.2

Rosemary Sea Bream

Prep time: 12 minutes , Cooking time: 20 minutes , Servings: 4

Ingredients:

- 1.5-pound sea bream fillet
- 1 tablespoon dried rosemary
- 1 teaspoon salt
- 2 tablespoons butter
- 1 teaspoon coconut oil
- 3 tablespoons chicken stock
- 1 teaspoon apple cider vinegar

Directions:

1. Rub the sea bream fillet with the salt and dried rosemary.
2. After this, sprinkle the fish with the apple cider vinegar and let it marinate for 10 minutes.
3. Meanwhile, preheat Ninja Foodi on Saute/Stear mode.
4. Add butter and coconut oil. Melt the mixture.
5. Then place the fish inside.
6. Add chicken stock.
7. Close the lid and cook the fish for 20 minutes on Saute/Stear mode.
8. When the fish is cooked – it will be very soft. Use the air crisp mode if you like crispy surface.
9. Enjoy!

Nutrition value/serving: calories 470, fat 17.1, fiber 0.4, carbs 0.6, protein 72.1

Calamari Rings

Prep time: 8 minutes , Cooking time: 6 minutes , Servings: 5

Ingredients:

- 1-pound calamari, trimmed, peeled
- ½ teaspoon salt
- ½ teaspoon ground white pepper
- ¼ cup almond flour
- 1 egg, whisked
- 1 teaspoon coconut oil

Directions:

1. Cut the calamari into the rings.
2. Then mix up together the almond flour, white pepper, and salt.
3. Dip the calamari rings into the whisked egg.
4. Then coat the calamari rings into the almond flour mixture.
5. Preheat Ninja Foodi on Air Crisp mode at 400 F.
6. Then place the calamari rings on the trivet and lower the air fryer lid.
7. Cook the meal for 6 minutes at 400 F.
8. Serve the calamari rings hot!

Nutrition value/serving: calories 115, fat 5.7, fiber 0.6, carbs 7.3, protein 7.8

Marinated Octopus Bites

Prep time: 8 minutes , Cooking time: 6 minutes , Servings: 3

Ingredients:
- 10 oz octopus
- 1 teaspoon low-sodium soy sauce
- ½ teaspoon ground cumin
- ½ teaspoon salt
- 1 tablespoon coconut oil
- 4 tablespoons coconut flakes

Directions:
1. Cut the octopus into the serving pieces.
2. Mix up together the octopus pieces, low-sodium soy sauce, salt, and coconut oil.
3. Make a shake and leave the seafood for 10 minutes to marinate.
4. After this, remove the octopus from the liquid and cover every piece into the coconut flakes.
5. Place the octopus bites in the pot and lower the Air fryer lid.
6. Cook the seafood for 9 minutes at 390 F.
7. Serve the cooked meal with your favorite Keto dip. Taste it!

Nutrition value/serving: calories 220, fat 8.8, fiber 0.6, carbs 5.4, protein 28.6

Bacon Pork

Prep time: 10 minutes , Cooking time: 47 minutes , Servings: 4

Ingredients:
- 1-pound pork loin
- 4 oz bacon, sliced
- 1 teaspoon salt
- ½ teaspoon cayenne pepper
- ½ teaspoon dried basil
- 1 tablespoon butter
- 3 tablespoons heavy cream
- ½ cup water, for cooking

Directions:
1. Melt the butter and stir together the dried basil, butter, heavy cream, cayenne pepper, and salt.
2. Then brush the pork loin with the butter mixture from each side.
3. Wrap the pork loin in bacon carefully.
4. Pour water in Ninja Foodi and insert rack.
5. Place the pork in the rack and close the lid.
6. Seal the lead and select PRESSURE mode (High).
7. Cook the pork loin for 40 minutes.
8. Then make the quick pressure release for 5 minutes.
9. After this, remove all the liquid from the pot and close the lid.
10. Set BROIL and cook the meal for 7 minutes more.
11. Slice it and serve!

Nutrition value/serving: calories 493, fat 34.7, fiber 0.1, carbs 0.9, protein 41.8

Beef Jerky

Prep time: 10 minutes , Cooking time: 6 hours , Servings: 4

Ingredients:

- 1-pound beef eye on round
- 1 teaspoon onion powder
- 1 teaspoon garlic powder
- 1 teaspoon ground black pepper
- 1 tablespoon low-sodium soy sauce
- 1 teaspoon Erythritol

Directions:

1. Mix up together all the spices and Erythritol.
2. Then slice the beef and sprinkle it with the low-sodium sauce and sprinkle well with the spice mixture.
3. Leave it to marinate for 2-3 hours.
4. After this, place the meat on the rack of Ninja Foodi, lower the air fryer lid.
5. Set Air Crisp mode for 160 F and cook the meat for 6 hours.
6. Serve it!

Nutrition value/serving: calories 198, fat 5.6, fiber 0.2, carbs 2.6, protein 33.4

Glazed Cod

Prep time: 10 minutes , Cooking time: 9 minutes , Servings: 2

Ingredients:

- 14 oz cod fillet, skinless
- 1 teaspoon coconut oil
- 1 teaspoon Erythritol
- 1 teaspoon butter
- 1 teaspoon ground thyme
- 1 teaspoon apple cider vinegar
- 1 teaspoon ground cumin
- 1 cup water, for cooking

Directions:

1. Churn together butter, coconut oil, apple cider vinegar, ground cumin, ground thyme, Erythritol. Pour water in Ninja Foodi.
2. Place the fish on the rack and close the lid. Seal it.
3. Cook the fish on Pressure mode for 3 minutes (High pressure).
4. Then make a quick pressure release and remove all the liquid from the pot.
5. Brush the cod fillet with the butter mixture from both sides.
6. Place the cod on the rack and set BROIL for 6 minutes.
7. Turn the fish into another side after 3 minutes of cooking.
8. Serve it hot!

Nutrition value/serving: calories 202, fat 6.2, fiber 0.3, carbs 2.8, protein 35.7

Cauliflower Mini Pizza

Prep time: 10 minutes , Cooking time: 11 minutes , Servings: 4

Ingredients:
- ½ pound cauliflower head, cut into the steaks
- 4 oz Mozzarella, sliced
- 3 oz Chorizo, sliced
- ½ teaspoon dried basil
- 4 teaspoon cream cheese
- ½ teaspoon cayenne pepper

Directions:
1. Churn together butter, coconut oil, apple cider vinegar, ground cumin, ground thyme, Erythritol. Pour water in Ninja Foodi.
2. Place the cauliflower steaks on the rack and insert it in Ninja Foodi.
3. Top the cauliflower steaks with chorizo and cream cheese.
4. Then add Mozzarella and sprinkle with cayenne pepper and dried basil.
5. Lower the air fryer lid and set Air Crisp mode.
6. Cook pizzas for 7 minutes at 390 F.
7. Then check the pizzas and cook them for 4 minutes more.
8. Serve it!

Nutrition value/serving: calories 203, fat 14.4, fiber 1.5, carbs 4.6, protein 14.5

Avocado Salad

Prep time: 10 minutes , Cooking time: 7 minutes , Servings: 4

Ingredients:
- 1 avocado, chopped
- 1 tablespoon lemon juice
- 1 teaspoon olive oil
- 10 oz chicken fillet, chopped
- ¼ cup heavy cream
- 1 tablespoon butter
- 1 teaspoon salt
- 1 teaspoon curry paste

Directions:
1. Mix up together the chicken fillet and curry paste.
2. Add salt and butter. Transfer the poultry in the pot of Ninja Foodi.
3. Add heavy cream and close the lid.
4. Seal the lid and select Pressure (High pressure).
5. Cook the chicken for 7 minutes. Then make a quick pressure release.
6. Transfer the cooked chicken in the bowl and chill till the room temperature.
7. Add chopped avocado and lemon juice.
8. Stir the salad and serve immediately!

Nutrition value/serving: calories 308, fat 22.6, fiber 3.4, carbs 5, protein 21.7

Desserts

Blackberry Cake

Prep time: 8 minutes , Cooking time: 25 minutes , Servings: 4

Ingredients:

- 4 tablespoons butter
- 3 tablespoon Erythritol
- 2 eggs, whisked
- ½ teaspoon vanilla extract
- 1 oz blackberries
- 1 cup almond flour
- ½ teaspoon baking powder

Directions:

1. Combine together all the liquid ingredients.
2. Then add baking powder, almond flour, and Erythritol.
3. Stir the mixture until smooth.
4. Add blackberries and stir the batter gently with the help of the spoon.
5. Take the non-sticky springform pan and transfer the batter inside.
6. Place the springform pan in the pot and lower the air fryer lid.
7. Cook the cake for 20 minutes at 365 F.
8. When the time is over – check the doneness of the cake with the help of the toothpick and cook for 5 minutes more if needed.
9. Chill it little and serve!

Nutrition value/serving: calories 173, fat 16.7, fiber 1.1, carbs 2.2, protein 4.2

Tender Pudding

Prep time: 10 minutes , Cooking time: 25 minutes , Servings: 4

Ingredients:

- 3 eggs, whisked
- ½ teaspoon vanilla extract
- 4 tablespoons pumpkin puree
- 1 teaspoon pumpkin pie spices
- 1 cup heavy cream
- 2 tablespoon Erythritol
- 1 cup water, for cooking

Directions:

1. Whisk together the eggs, vanilla extract, pumpkin puree, pumpkin pie spices, cream, and Erythritol.
2. Pour the liquid into the non-sticky cake pan.
3. Pour water in the pot.
4. Place the pudding in a cake pan in the pot on the rack and close the lid.
5. Select Steam mode and cook the dessert for 25 minutes.
6. Let the cooked pudding rest for 10 minutes (open Foodi lid).
7. Place it in the fridge for a minimum of 4 hours.
8. Enjoy!

Nutrition value/serving: calories 159, fat 14.5, fiber 0.5, carbs 2.7, protein 5

Mini Cheesecakes

Prep time: 30 minutes , Cooking time: 4 minutes , Servings: 4

Ingredients:

- 8 tablespoons cream cheese
- 4 tablespoon Erythritol
- 2 tablespoons heavy cream
- ½ teaspoon vanilla extract
- 4 tablespoons almond flour

Directions:

1. Whisk together the cream cheese and heavy cream.
2. When the mixture is smooth – add 1 tablespoon of Erythritol and stir until homogenous.
3. After this, add vanilla extract and stir again.
4. Scoop the medium balls from the cream cheese mixture.
5. Mix up together the almond flour and all the remaining Erythritol.
6. Then coat every cheesecake ball into the almond flour mixture.
7. Freeze the balls for 20 minutes or until they are solid.
8. Place the cheesecake balls in the Ninja Foodi basket and lower the air fryer lid.
9. Cook the dessert at 400 F for 4 minutes.
10. When the time is over – serve the dessert immediately.
11. Taste it!

Nutrition value/serving: calories 139, fat 13.1, fiber 0.8, carbs 2.3, protein 3.2

Avocado Mousse

Prep time: 10 minutes , Cooking time: 2 minutes , Servings: 7

Ingredients:

- 2 avocado, peeled, cored
- 1 teaspoon of cocoa powder
- 1/3 cup heavy cream
- 1 teaspoon butter
- 3 tablespoons Erythritol
- 1 teaspoon vanilla extract

Directions:

1. Preheat Ninja Foodi at "Saute/Stear" mode for 5 minutes.
2. Meanwhile, mash the avocado until smooth and mix it up with Erythritol.
3. Place the butter in the pot and melt.
4. Add mashed avocado mixture and stir well.
5. Add cocoa powder and stir until homogenous. Saute the mixture for 3 minutes.
6. Meanwhile, whisk the heavy cream on high speed for 2 minutes.
7. Transfer the cooked avocado mash in the bowl and chill in ice water.
8. When the avocado mash reaches room temperature – add whisked heavy cream and vanilla extract. Stir gently to get white-chocolate swirls.
9. Transfer the mousse into small cups and chill for 4 hours in the fridge.
10. Serve!

Nutrition value/serving: calories 144, fat 13.9, fiber 3.9, carbs 10.5, protein 1.3

Keto Brownie Batter

Prep time: 10 minutes , Cooking time: 5 minutes , Servings: 5

Ingredients:
- 1/3 cup almond flour
- 1 tablespoon Erythritol
- ¼ cup heavy cream
- ½ teaspoon vanilla extract
- 3 tablespoons cocoa powder
- 3 tablespoons butter
- 1 oz dark chocolate

Directions:
1. Place the almond flour in the springform pan and flatten to make the layer.
2. Then place the springform pan in the pot and lower the air fryer lid.
3. Cook the almond flour for 3 minutes at 400 F or until the almond flour gets a golden color.
4. Meanwhile, combine together cocoa powder and heavy cream; whisk the heavy cream until smooth.
5. Add vanilla extract and Erythritol.
6. Remove the almond flour from Ninja Foodi and chill well.
7. Toss butter and dark chocolate in the pot and preheat for 1 minute on Saute/Stear mode.
8. When the butter is soft – add it in the heavy cream mixture.
9. Then add chocolate and almond flour.
10. Stir the mass until homogenous and serve!

Nutrition value/serving: calories 159, fat 14.9, fiber 2.1, carbs 9, protein 2.5

Almond Bites

Prep time: 10 minutes , Cooking time: 14 minutes , Servings: 5

Ingredients:
- 1 egg, whisked
- 1 cup almond flour
- ¼ cup almond milk
- 1 tablespoon coconut flakes
- ½ teaspoon vanilla extract
- ½ teaspoon baking powder
- ½ teaspoon apple cider vinegar
- 2 tablespoons butter

Directions:
1. Mix up together the whisked egg, almond milk, apple cider vinegar, baking powder, vanilla extract, and butter.
2. Stir the mixture and add almond flour and coconut flakes. Knead the dough.
3. If the dough is sticky – add more almond flour.
4. Make the medium balls from the dough and place them on the rack of Ninja Foodi.
5. Press them gently with the hand palm.
6. Lower the air fryer lid and cook the dessert for 12 minutes at 360 F.
7. Check if the dessert is cooked – and cook for 2 minutes more for a crunchy crust.
8. Enjoy!

Nutrition value/serving: calories 118, fat 11.5, fiber 1, carbs 2.4, protein 2.7

Keto Donuts

Prep time: 20 minutes , Cooking time: 10 minutes , Servings: 5

Ingredients:
- 1 ½ cup almond flour
- ½ teaspoon baking soda
- 1 teaspoon vanilla extract
- 1 egg, whisked
- 2 tablespoons Erythritol
- ½ cup heavy cream

Directions:
1. Mix up together the whisked egg, heavy cream, Erythritol, vanilla extract, and baking soda.
2. When the mixture is homogenous – add almond flour. Stir well and knead the non-sticky dough.
3. Let the dough rest for 10 minutes.
4. After this, roll up the dough with the help of the rolling pin into 1 inch thick.
5. Then make the donuts with the help of the cutter.
6. Set the Ninja Foodi Bake mode + Roast option and set 360 F.
7. When the appliance is preheated – place the donuts in the basket and lower the air fryer lid.
8. Cook the donuts for 5 minutes.
9. Chill the donuts well and serve!

Nutrition value/serving: calories 118, fat 11.5, fiber 1, carbs 2.4, protein 2.7

Pumpkin Pie

Prep time: 10 minutes , Cooking time: 25 minutes , Servings: 6

Ingredients:
- 1 tablespoon pumpkin puree
- 1 cup coconut flour
- ½ teaspoon baking powder
- 1 teaspoon apple cider vinegar
- 1 teaspoon Pumpkin spices
- 1 tablespoon butter
- ¼ cup heavy cream
- 2 tablespoon liquid stevia
- 1 egg, whisked

Directions:
1. Melt the butter and combine it together with the heavy cream, apple cider vinegar, liquid stevia, egg, and baking powder.
2. Add pumpkin puree and coconut flour.
3. After this, add pumpkin spices and stir the batter until smooth.
4. Pour the batter in Ninja Foodi basket and lower the air fryer lid.
5. Set the "Bake" mode 360 F.
6. Cook the pie for 25 minutes.
7. When the time is over – let the pie chill till the room temperature. Serve it!

Nutrition value/serving: calories 127, fat 6.6, fiber 8.1, carbs 14.2, protein 3.8

Chocolate Cakes

Prep time: 10 minutes , Cooking time: 22 minutes , Servings: 3

Ingredients:

- 1 tablespoon cocoa powder
- 4 tablespoons almond flour
- ½ teaspoon vanilla extract
- 1 tablespoon Truvia
- 1/3 cup heavy cream
- ¼ teaspoon baking powder
- Cooking spray

Directions:

1. Mix up together the cocoa powder, almond flour, vanilla extract, Truvia, heavy cream, and baking powder.
2. Use the mixer to make the smooth batter.
3. Spray the silicone molds with the cooking spray inside.
4. Pour the batter into the silicone molds and transfer then in Ninja Foodi basket.
5. Close the air fryer lid and set Bake-Roast Option.
6. Cook the cakes at 255 F for 22 minutes.
7. Serve the dessert chilled!

Nutrition value/serving: calories 108, fat 9.6, fiber 1.6, carbs 5.2, protein 2.6

Keto Brownie

Prep time: 10 minutes , Cooking time: 32 minutes , Servings: 6

Ingredients:

- 3 tablespoons Truvia
- 1 oz sugar-free chocolate chips
- 2 eggs, whisked
- ½ teaspoon vanilla extract
- 3 tablespoon butter, melted
- 1 tablespoon almond flour

Directions:

1. Whisk together the melted butter, almond flour, vanilla extract, and Truvia.
2. Melt the chocolate chips and add them in the butter mixture.
3. Add eggs and stir until smooth.
4. Pour the batter into Ninja Foodi basket (Bake mode) and cook at 360 F for 32 minutes.
5. Then check if the brownie cooked and chill well.
6. Cut it into the servings and serve!

Nutrition value/serving: calories 99, fat 8.8, fiber 0.1, carbs 5.9, protein 2.4

Lava Cups

Prep time: 6 minutes , Cooking time: 8 minutes , Servings: 2

Ingredients:
- 2 eggs, whisked
- 3 tablespoons flax meal
- 2 teaspoon of cocoa powder
- ½ teaspoon baking powder
- 2 tablespoons heavy cream
- Cooking spray

Directions:
1. Spray the cake cups with the cooking spray inside.
2. Mix up together all the remaining ingredients and pour the mixture into the prepared cups.
3. Cover the cups with foil and place in Ninja Foodi.
4. Set the Bake mode 355 F.
5. Close the lid and cook the dessert for 8 minutes.
6. Serve the cooked lava cups hot!

Nutrition value/serving: calories 165, fat 13.9, fiber 3.6, carbs 5.3, protein 8.4

Coconut Pie

Prep time: 6 minutes , Cooking time: 10 minutes , Servings: 4

Ingredients:
- 1 tablespoon coconut flour
- 5 oz coconut, shredded
- ½ teaspoon vanilla extract
- 1 tablespoon Truvia
- 1 teaspoon butter
- 1 egg, whisked
- ¼ cup heavy cream

Directions:
1. Mix up together the coconut flour, coconut shred, and butter.
2. Stir the mixture until homogenous.
3. Add whisked egg, vanilla extract, Truvia, and heavy cream. Stir well.
4. Transfer the pie mixture into the basket and lower the air fryer lid.
5. Set the Bake mode 355F.
6. Cook the pie for 10 minutes.
7. Check if the pie is cooked with the help of the toothpick and chill it till the room temperature.
8. Serve it!

Nutrition value/serving: calories 185, fat 16.9, fiber 3.9, carbs 8.2, protein 3

Peanut Butter Cookies

Prep time: 10 minutes , Cooking time: 11 minutes , Servings: 7

Ingredients:
- 1 tablespoon Truvia
- 1 egg, whisked
- 6 oz cashew butter

Directions:
1. Mix up together all the ingredients and make the small balls.
2. Place the balls in the basket of Ninja Foodi and close the lid.
3. Set the Bake mode and cook the cookies at 330 F for 11 minutes.
4. Increase the time of cooking if you like crunchy cookies.
5. Serve!

Nutrition value/serving: calories 152, fat 12.6, fiber 0.5, carbs 7.4, protein 5.1

Ginger Cookies

Prep time: 10 minutes , Cooking time: 14 minutes , Servings: 7

Ingredients:
- 1 cup almond flour
- 3 tablespoons butter
- 1 egg
- ½ teaspoon baking powder
- 3 tablespoon Erythritol
- 1 teaspoon ground ginger
- ½ teaspoon ground cinnamon
- 3 tablespoons heavy cream

Directions:
1. Beat the egg in the bowl and whisk it gently.
2. Add baking powder, Erythritol, ground ginger, ground cinnamon, heavy cream, and flour.
3. Stir gently and add butter,
4. Knead the non-sticky dough.
5. Roll up the dough with the help of the rolling pin and make the cookies with the help of the cutter.
6. Place the cookies in the basket in one layer and close the lid.
7. Set the Bake mode and cook the cookies for 14 minutes at 350 F.
8. When the cookies are cooked – let them chill well and serve!

Nutrition value/serving: calories 172, fat 15.6, fiber 1.8, carbs 4.1, protein 4.4

Vanilla Creme Brulee

Prep time: 20 minutes , Cooking time: 10 minutes , Servings: 3

Ingredients:
- 1 cup heavy cream
- 4 egg yolks
- 3 tablespoons Truvia
- ½ teaspoon vanilla extract

Directions:
1. Whisk together the egg yolks and 2 tablespoons of Truvia.
2. Add heavy cream and stir until homogenous.
3. Place the mixture into the ramekins and cover them with the foil.
4. Make the small holes on the top of the foil with the help of the toothpick.
5. Pour ½ cup of water in Ninja Foofi basket and insert trivet.
6. Place the ramekins on the trivet and close the pressure cooker lid.
7. Cook the dessert on Pressure mode (High pressure) for 10 minutes.
8. Then make the quick pressure release for 5 minutes.
9. Let the dessert chill for 10 minutes.
10. Remove the foil from the ramekins and sprinkle the surface of creme brulee with Truvia.
11. Use the hand torch to caramelize the surface.
12. Serve it!

Nutrition value/serving: calories 212, fat 20.8, fiber 0, carbs 6.7, protein 4.4

Cinnamon Bun

Prep time: 10 minutes , Cooking time: 15 minutes , Servings: 8

Ingredients:
- 1 cup almond flour
- ½ teaspoon baking powder
- 3 tablespoon Erythritol
- 2 tablespoon ground cinnamon
- ½ teaspoon vanilla extract
- 1 tablespoon butter
- 1 egg, whisked
- ¾ teaspoon salt
- ¼ cup almond milk

Directions:
1. Mix up together the almond flour, baking powder, vanilla extract, egg, salt, and almond milk.
2. Knead the soft and non-sticky dough.
3. Roll up the dough with the help of the rolling pin.
4. Sprinkle dough with the butter, cinnamon, and Erythritol.
5. Roll the dough into the log.
6. Cut the roll into 7 pieces.
7. Spray Ninja Foodi basket with the cooking spray.
8. Place the cinnamon buns in the basket and close the lid.
9. Set the Bake mode and cook the buns for 15 minutes at 355 F.
10. Check if the buns are cooked with the help of the toothpick.
11. Chill the buns well and serve!

Nutrition value/serving: calories 127, fat 10.5, fiber 3, carbs 9.2, protein 4

Chip Cookies

Prep time: 10 minutes , Cooking time: 9 minutes , Servings: 8

Ingredients:
- 1 oz sugar-free chocolate chips
- 3 tablespoon butter
- 1 cup almond flour
- 1 egg, whisked
- 2 tablespoons Erythritol

Directions:
1. Mix up together the almond flour and whisked the egg.
2. Add butter and Erythritol, and mix up the mixture until homogenous.
3. Add chocolate chips and knead the homogenous dough.
4. Make 8 small balls from the dough and transfer them on the rack of Ninja Foodi.
5. Close the air fryer lid and set Bake mode.
6. Cook the chip cookies for 9 minutes at 360 F.
7. Chill the cookies and serve!

Nutrition value/serving: calories 145, fat 12.3, fiber 1.5, carbs 8.4, protein 3.9

Raspberry Dump Cake

Prep time: 10 minutes , Cooking time: 30 minutes , Servings: 10

Ingredients:
- 1 ½ cup coconut flour
- 1 teaspoon baking powder
- 1 teaspoon lemon juice
- ½ cup raspberries
- ¼ cup Erythritol
- 1 egg, whisked
- 1/3 cup almond milk
- 1 tablespoon butter, melted
- ½ teaspoon vanilla extract

Directions:
1. Combine together all the dry ingredients.
2. Then add egg, almond milk, and butter.
3. Add vanilla extract and lemon juice.
4. Stir the mixture well. You have to get a liquid batter.
5. Place the layer of the raspberries in the silicone mold.
6. Pour batter over the raspberries.
7. Place the mold on the rack and insert it into Ninja Foodi basket.
8. Close the air fryer lid and set Bake mode.
9. Cook the cake for 30 minutes at 350 F.
10. When the cake is cooked – chill it well.
11. Turn upside down and transfer on the serving plate.
12. Enjoy!

Nutrition value/serving: calories 107, fat 4.5, fiber 8.9, carbs 15.1, protein 4.3

Pumpkin Muffins

Prep time: 7 minutes , Cooking time: 20 minutes , Servings: 5

Ingredients:
- 1 tablespoon butter, melted
- 1 tablespoon pumpkin puree
- 1 teaspoon ground cinnamon
- ¼ teaspoon ground ginger
- 1 egg, beaten
- 3 tablespoon Erythritol
- ½ cup almond flour
- ½ teaspoon baking powder

Directions:
1. Mix up together all the ingredients in the mixing bowl.
2. Stir the mixture well until smooth.
3. Transfer the mixture into the silicone muffin molds and place on the track in Ninja Foodi.
4. Lower the air fryer lid and set Bake mode.
5. Cook the muffins for 20 minutes at 330 F.
6. When the time is over – let the muffins rest little and serve!

Nutrition value/serving: calories 52, fat 4.6, fiber 0.7, carbs 8.7, protein 1.8

Cinnamon Bites

Prep time: 10 minutes , Cooking time: 12 minutes , Servings: 5

Ingredients:
- 1 teaspoon ground cinnamon
- 1 cup almond flour
- ½ teaspoon baking powder
- 1 teaspoon olive oil
- ¼ cup almond milk
- 1 teaspoon butter
- ½ teaspoon vanilla extract
- 1 cup water, for cooking

Directions:
1. Combine together all the dry ingredients.
2. Then add butter and almond milk in the dry ingredients.
3. Add vanilla extract and olive oil and knead the smooth and non-sticky dough.
4. Make the medium balls from the dough and place them in the silicone molds.
5. Pour water in Ninja Foodi basket.
6. Place the molds on the rack in Ninja Foodi.
7. Close the lid and seal it.
8. Set Pressure mode (High pressure)
9. Cook the cinnamon bites for 10 minutes.
10. Then make natural pressure release for 10 minutes.
11. Then remove the liquid from the basket and lower the air fryer lid.
12. Set Air Crisp and cook the bites for 2 minutes more.
13. Serve !

Nutrition value/serving: calories 180, fat 15.2, fiber 2.9, carbs 6.1, protein 5.1

Pecan Muffins

Prep time: 10 minutes , Cooking time: 12 minutes , Servings: 6

Ingredients:
- 4 tablespoon butter, softened
- 4 tablespoon coconut flour
- 1 egg, whisked
- 4 tablespoon heavy cream
- ½ teaspoon vanilla extract
- 1 tablespoon pecans, crushed
- 2 tablespoon Erythritol

Directions:
1. In the mixing bowl combine together the coconut flour, softened butter, whisked egg, heavy cream, vanilla extract, and Erythritol.
2. Use the hand mixer to mix up the mixture until smooth.
3. Pour the smooth batter in the silicone muffin molds.
4. Top every muffin with the pecans and transfer in Ninja Foodi rack.
5. Lower the air fryer lid and set Bake mode.
6. Cook the muffins for 12 minutes at 350 F.
7. Check if the muffins are cooked and transfer on the plate. Chill well and serve!

Nutrition value/serving: calories 170, fat 15.1, fiber 3.6, carbs 11.1, protein 2.8

Vanilla Muffins

Prep time: 7 minutes , Cooking time: 2 minutes , Servings: 4

Ingredients:
- 4 tablespoon coconut flour
- 1 teaspoon coconut shred
- 1 teaspoon vanilla extract
- 1 egg, beaten
- 1 tablespoon Truvia
- ¼ teaspoon baking powder
- 1 cup water, for cooking

Directions:
1. Mix up together all the ingredients and stir well until you get a thick batter.
2. Add water in the Ninja Foodi basket.
3. Place the batter into the muffin molds and transfer them on the Ninja Foodi rack.
4. Lower the pressure cooker lid and set Pressure mode (High pressure).
5. Cook the muffins for 2 minutes. Use the quick pressure release method.
6. Chill the muffins and serve!

Nutrition value/serving: calories 61, fat 2.9, fiber 3.3, carbs 7, protein 2.5

Sweet Zucchini Crisp

Prep time: 5 minutes , Cooking time: 10 minutes , Servings: 4

Ingredients:
- 1 zucchini, chopped
- 1 teaspoon Vanilla extract
- 2 tablespoon Erythritol
- 1 tablespoon coconut flakes
- 2 tablespoon butter
- 1 tablespoon almond flour

Directions:
1. Preheat Ninja Foodi at Saute/Stear mode for 5 minutes at 360 F.
2. Toss the butter in the Ninja Foodi basket.
3. Add chopped zucchini and saute the vegetables for 3 minutes.
4. Add vanilla extract, coconut flakes, Erythritol, and stir well.
5. Cook the zucchini for 4 minutes more.
6. Then add almond flour and stir well.
7. Saute the dessert for 1 minute.
8. Use the Air crips mode for 2 minutes to get a crunchy crust.
9. Serve the cooked dessert immediately!

Nutrition value/serving: calories 84, fat 8.5, fiber 0.5, carbs 6.1, protein 0.3

Mint Cake

Prep time: 8 minutes , Cooking time: 62 minutes , Servings: 6

Ingredients:
- 1 teaspoon dried mint
- 1 cup coconut flour
- 1 teaspoon baking powder
- ¼ cup Erythritol
- 2 eggs, whisked
- ¼ cup heavy cream
- 1 tablespoon butter
- ½ teaspoon lemon zest, grated

Directions:
1. In the mixing bowl mix up together all the ingredients.
2. Use the cooking machine to make the soft batter from the mixture.
3. Pour the batter in the Ninja Foodie basket and flatten it well.
4. Close the pressure cooker lid and set Pressure mode. Seal the lid.
5. Cook the cake on Low pressure for 55 minutes.
6. Then lower the air fryer lid and set Air Crisp mode.
7. Cook the cake for 7 minutes more at 400 F.
8. Chill the cake well and serve!

Nutrition value/serving: calories 136, fat 7.2, fiber 8.1, carbs 22, protein 4.7

Vanilla Custard

Prep time: 5 minutes , Cooking time: 10 minutes , Servings: 4

Ingredients:
- 3 egg yolks
- 1 cup almond milk
- 1 teaspoon vanilla extract
- 2 tablespoon Truvia

Directions:
1. Whisk together egg yolk and Truvia.
2. Add vanilla extract and almond milk.
3. Preheat Ninja Foodi at Saute/Stear mode at 365F for 5 minutes
4. Then pour the almond milk mixture and saute it for 10 minutes.
5. Stir the liquid all the time.
6. When the liquid start to be thick – transfer it into the serving jars and leave it for 1 hour in the fridge.
7. Serve it!

Nutrition value/serving: calories 181, fat 17.7, fiber 1.3, carbs 6.2, protein 3.4

CPSIA information can be obtained
at www.ICGtesting.com
Printed in the USA
LVHW021758050121
675799LV00033B/759

9 781637 331316